THE FOUR WOMEN OF THE APOCALYPSE

Dr. CJ Walker

ISBN-13: 979-8-9925440-0-8

I dedicate this first endeavor at a study booklet to my church family, whom I have the privilege of serving in Christ. This study was prepared with you in mind, that you might grow deeper in your knowledge of Scripture and stronger in your walk with the Lord. May this work be a blessing to you, as you continue to seek His truth and live for His glory.

"For this cause we also, since the day we heard it, do not cease to pray for you, and to desire that ye might be filled with the knowledge of his will in all wisdom and spiritual understanding; That ye might walk worthy of the Lord unto all pleasing, being fruitful in every good work, and increasing in the knowledge of God."

—Colossians 1:9–10

CONTENTS

Foreword

In every generation, the church is called to grow in the grace and knowledge of our Lord Jesus Christ, anchoring itself in the unchanging truth of God's Word. This study on The Four Women of the Apocalypse was developed to guide believers toward a richer understanding of key passages in the Book of Revelation. Originally presented in our Midweek Bible Study and Prayer Meetings, these lessons were designed to strengthen our church's grasp of biblical prophecy and promote practical application.

I do not claim originality for many of the insights presented here, as this study builds upon the faithful exegesis of others. Throughout this study, I have sought to give due credit where I have gleaned from the wisdom of others, recognizing that the truths of Scripture are not new but must be continually rediscovered and applied. My role has been to organize and present these materials in a way that would be edifying for our church family—and now, through this printed study, for others who may find it beneficial.

Each lesson seeks careful observation, interpretation, and application of the biblical text, with thought-provoking questions for diligent study. An appendix has been included with expository outlines from sermons preached on these passages in our church plant.

It is my prayer that the Holy Spirit will use this study to illuminate the Scriptures, strengthen your faith, and equip you to rightly divide the Word of God. May it encourage you to walk more closely with the Lord and live with a greater awareness of His unfolding plan.

To God be the glory,
Pastor Walker

CHAPTER ONE

Jezebel of Thyatira

Introduction

"And unto the angel of the church in Thyatira write; These things saith the Son of God, who hath his eyes like unto a flame of fire, and his feet are like fine brass;"

The Book of Revelation introduces four women, each symbolizing something greater than themselves. A study of these women and their significance can be organized into four key sections: Jezebel of Thyatira, the Sun-clothed Woman, the Great Harlot, and the Bride and Wife of the Messiah. The first of these four women is Jezebel. The seven churches mentioned in the Book of Revelation represent seven distinct periods in the history of the visible church. This particular passage corresponds to the Dark Ages, which lasted from 600 to 1517.

1. Who was telling John to write down this vision? (2:18)

____

____

2. How did the speaker in this passage identify Himself? (2:18)

____

____

I. Christ's Message to Thyatira — (Rev. 2:18a)

The letter is addressed to the angel of the church in Thyatira. Interestingly, the name Thyatira in Greek means "continual" or "perpetual sacrifice," which aptly characterizes the church during the Dark Ages. This was when the Roman Catholic doctrine of the "continual sacrifice" in the mass emerged and became central to its teachings.

II. The Messiah's Authority and Insight — (Rev. 2:18b)

Each letter to the churches describes the Messiah, and in this case, Jesus is portrayed as the Son of God, with eyes like a flame of fire and feet like burnished brass. These vivid symbols point to judgment, emphasizing that He is preparing to judge this particular church.

3. What would be good or bad about having the ability to read others' minds? Why?

____

____

4. What are the three best habits you have?

____

____

5. What does it mean that Christ's eyes were "like blazing fire"?

____

____

III. The Commendation: Recognizing Good Works — (Rev. 2:19)

> *"I know thy works, and charity, and service, and faith, and thy patience, and thy works; and the last to be more than the first."*

The church is commended for its good works and accomplishments. These efforts are recognized and appreciated; they are not without value in the eyes of the Lord.

6. For what did Christ praise the church at Thyatira? (2:19)

____

____

7. What value is there in choosing to remain ignorant of certain evil ideas and practices?

____

____

8. What is the impact of the first two words of verse 19?

____

____

IV. The Condemnation: Jezebel's Influence Exposed — (Rev. 2:20–23)

At this point, the first woman (metaphorically, the Spiritual Adulteress), Jezebel, is introduced. This condemnation highlights two key issues: the church's toleration of Jezebel and the judgment that will come upon her.

9. What did Christ know about the church at Thyatira? (2:19)

____

____

10. What are some things people make idols (gods) of today?

____

____

A. The Tolerance of Jezebel's Sin — (Rev. 2:20)

"Notwithstanding I have a few things against thee, because thou sufferest that woman Jezebel, which calleth herself a

prophetess, to teach and to seduce my servants to commit fornication, and to eat things sacrificed unto idols."

It is unlikely that a woman named Jezebel caused trouble in the church at Thyatira. Jezebel is not a Greek name but a Phoenician one, and by this point in history, the Phoenicians had ceased to exist as a distinct ethnic group. Instead, the name Jezebel here likely refers to the infamous queen of the Old Testament, symbolically representing the church's spiritual condition at Thyatira. Jezebel was the Phoenician princess who married Ahab, king of Israel (1 Kings 16:29–33). She introduced Baal worship, a pagan religious system that led to widespread idolatry in the Northern Kingdom.

In the context of Thyatira, Jezebel represents Roman Catholicism during the Dark Ages. During this period, the church became heavily influenced by pagan practices, resulting in a religious system far removed from the New Testament model. This imagery suggests that paganism and false religious systems infiltrated the Church, resulting in spiritual idolatry or fornication. Numerous pagan elements had been introduced by the Dark Ages, creating a church that bore little resemblance to the pure and simple faith of the early believers.

11. For what did Christ chastise the church at Thyatira? (2:20)

____

____

12. What word identifies the church's sin (verse 20)?

____

____

13. What sins do we tend to tolerate in our own lives or in the lives of our Christian friends when we should not?

____

____

During this era, as rightly observed by Dr. Arnold Fruchtenbaum, ten significant false doctrines emerged in the Church:

1. *Baptismal Regeneration*: The belief is that baptism is essential for salvation, giving the ritual of sprinkling water unwarranted saving power.

2. *Justification by Works*: The teaching that salvation requires both grace through faith and good works contradicts the biblical doctrine of salvation by faith alone.

3. *The Worship of Images*: (i.e., The Iconography Debate) Although it is asserted that worship is directed at what the image symbolizes rather than the image itself, the act of bowing or crossing oneself before a statue undeniably constitutes idolatry, violating God's command against making and bowing to images.

4. *Clerical Celibacy*: The belief that celibacy enhances spirituality requires priests to remain unmarried and creates an unscriptural division between clergy and laity.

5. *Confessionalism*: The practice of confessing sins to a priest for absolution, whereas Scripture teaches confession should be made directly to God for sins against Him or to the person wronged.

6. *Purgatory*: The doctrine that the dead, if not fully qualified for Heaven or Hell, undergo a period of purging for their sins to become fit for Heaven, a concept absent from Scripture.

7. *Transubstantiation*: The teaching that the bread and wine of the Eucharist become the literal body and blood of Christ, re-sacrificing Him in the mass, contrary to the biblical truth that His sacrifice was once for all (Hebrews 10:10).

8. *The Selling of Indulgences*: The practice of purchasing indulgences to reduce time in purgatory for oneself or a deceased relative, turning forgiveness into a commodity.

9. *Penance*: The belief that self-inflicted suffering or bodily torment can atone for sin, undermining the sufficiency of Christ's atonement.

10. *Mariolatry*: The elevation of Mary to a sinless and divine status, including worship of her as the "Mother of God," a doctrine foreign to Scripture.

These doctrines reflect the tragic departure of the Church during the Dark Ages from the biblical gospel, replacing it with traditions and practices rooted in paganism and human invention. The figure of Jezebel vividly portrays this spiritual decline and the need for repentance and restoration.

14. "Fornication (i.e., immorality) … idols" (2:20). Why are these two sins often placed together in Scripture?

____

____

B. The Consequences of Jezebel's Judgment — (Rev. 2:21–23)

> *"And I gave her space to repent of her fornication; and she repented not. Behold, I will cast her into a bed, and them that commit adultery with her into great tribulation, except they repent of their deeds. And I will kill her children with death; and all the churches shall know that I am he which searcheth the reins and hearts: and I will give unto every one of you according to your works."*

The judgment pronounced on Jezebel is that she will be cast into the Great Tribulation, along with her children—those who adhere to the system she represents. This judgment reflects God's righteous response to the idolatry and corruption symbolized by Jezebel. While the true Church will be raptured before the Tribulation begins, this false church, represented by Jezebel, will remain on earth, endure the Tribulation, and ultimately face destruction as part of God's divine justice.

15. How did Christ show patience? (2:21)

____

____

16. "Her children" (2:23). Who does this refer to, if the name Jezebel is symbolic?

____

____

17. What judgments did the Son of God pronounce on the one He called Jezebel? (2:22–23)

____

____

18. What dangers do we face when we refuse to respond to God or repent of our sins?

____

---

19. When we are misled by others, what can we do to correct our mistakes? How?

---

20. When should we take responsibility for the errors of others in the church? How?

V. The Exhortation: Faithfulness in the Face of Evil — (Rev. 2:24–25)

> *"But unto you I say, and unto the rest in Thyatira, as many as have not this doctrine, and which have not known the depths of Satan, as they speak; I will put upon you none other burden. But that which ye have already hold fast till I come."*

The word of exhortation is directed to those who have not become part of the Jezebel system and who do not embrace the "deep things of Satan." Catholicism is presented here as a satanic counterfeit to the true teachings of the New Testament. The encouragement to these faithful believers is simple yet profound: they are to hold fast to the truth they have—the pure, unadulterated teachings of the New Testament. Remaining steadfast in this truth will require all their spiritual strength, especially given the challenging times in which they are living.

21. "*But . . . hold fast till I come*" (2:25) (Cf. verse 26.) What does this teach about Christian living?

---

22. What is the bright note?

23. What challenge did Christ give to those who resisted Jezebel's teaching and sinful behavior? (2:24–25)

24. What have you been tolerating in your life that you need to reject and change?

VI. The Promise to Overcomers — (Rev. 2:26–29)

"And he that overcometh, and keepeth my works unto the end, to him will I give power over the nations: And he shall rule them with a rod of iron; as the vessels of a potter shall they be broken to shivers: even as I received of my Father. And I will give him the morning star. He that hath an ear, let him hear what the Spirit saith unto the churches."

This promise is twofold: salvation and authority in the Messianic Kingdom. First, the promise of authority is found in Revelation 2:26–27: The overcomer—one who overcomes the influence of Jezebel—will be granted true authority during the Millennial Kingdom. This stands in stark contrast to the false authority practiced by this church.

25. "*Power over the nations*" (2:26). In what sense is this a reward to Christians enduring persecution, as they were in Asia those days?

Secondly, the promise of the Morning Star is given in Revelation 2:28–29: According to Revelation 22:16, the Morning Star represents the Messiah Himself:

"I Jesus have sent mine angel to testify unto you these things in the churches. I am the root and the offspring of David, and the bright and morning star."

Conclusion

Thus, the one who overcomes is the one who places their trust in the Messiah for salvation—trusting in Him alone rather than the ten false doctrines of Jezebel's system. Because they trust in Christ alone for their salvation, they are given the Morning Star, which is the Messiah Himself.

26. What two gifts were promised to "*him who overcometh*"? (2:26–28)

____

____

27. Why do you think "*overcome*" appears so often (14 times) in Revelation?

____

____

28. How did Jesus refer to God? (2:28)

____

____

39. In addition to the church at Thyatira, who else was commanded to pay heed to this message? (2:29)

____

____

30. What observations do you have on these pertinent cross references: 2 Peter 1:19; Revelation 22:16; Revelation 19:13–15?

____

____

CHAPTER TWO

The Sun-Clothed Woman

Introduction

The second woman described in this section symbolizes the nation of Israel. John's readers are introduced to her in this chapter, which metaphorically describes Israel during the Tribulation period. The chapter naturally breaks down into three key parts: a summary of Satan's persecution of Israel, the reason behind Satan's persecution of Israel, and the specific details of how Satan persecutes Israel. The first five verses outline Satan's persecution of Israel throughout history, while verse 6 shifts focus to the future, specifically the Great Tribulation. Verses 1–5 provide a historical overview.

1. How does it feel to be accused of something you didn't do?

____

____

2. What is the clearest example of the existence of Satan that you're aware of?

____

____

3. What observations do you have from the following related verses? Psalm

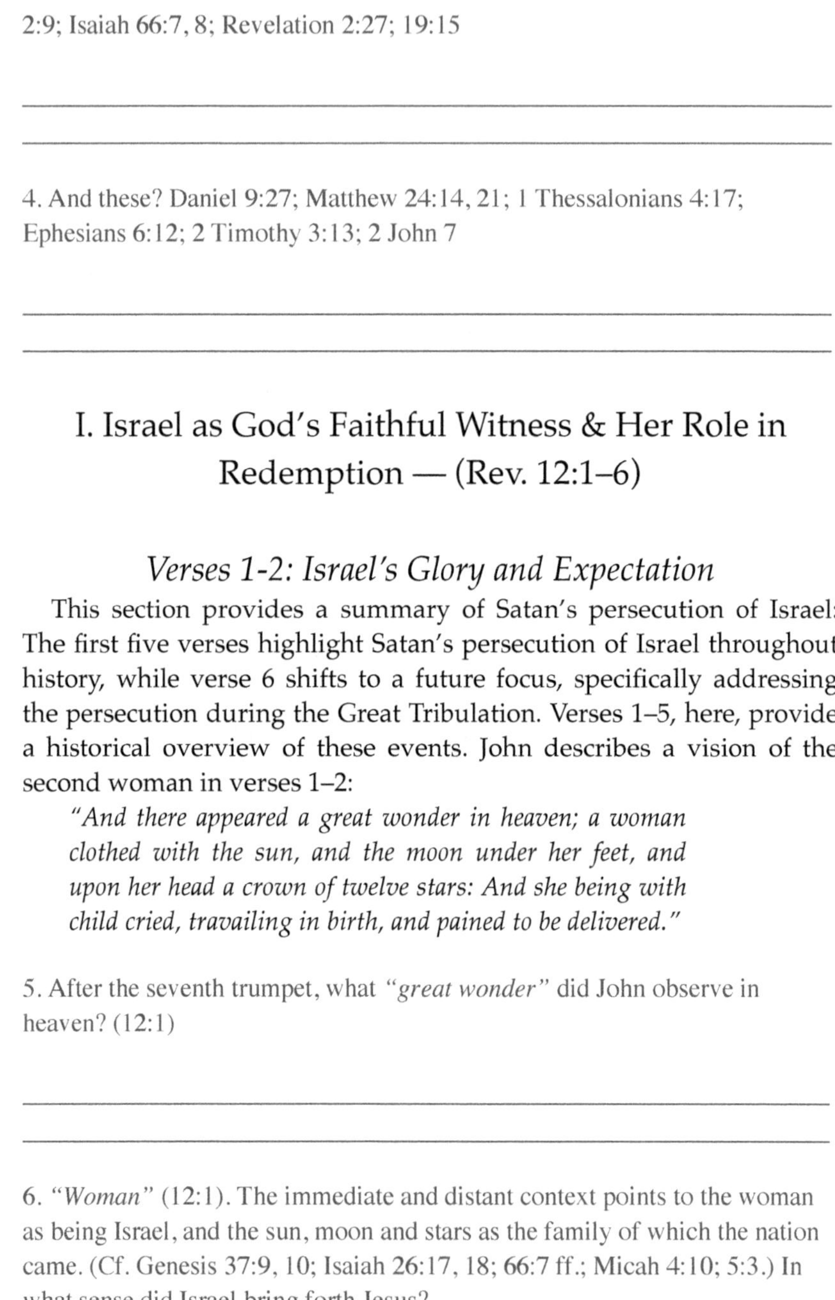

2:9; Isaiah 66:7, 8; Revelation 2:27; 19:15

4. And these? Daniel 9:27; Matthew 24:14, 21; 1 Thessalonians 4:17; Ephesians 6:12; 2 Timothy 3:13; 2 John 7

I. Israel as God's Faithful Witness & Her Role in Redemption — (Rev. 12:1–6)

Verses 1-2: Israel's Glory and Expectation

This section provides a summary of Satan's persecution of Israel: The first five verses highlight Satan's persecution of Israel throughout history, while verse 6 shifts to a future focus, specifically addressing the persecution during the Great Tribulation. Verses 1–5, here, provide a historical overview of these events. John describes a vision of the second woman in verses 1–2:

> *"And there appeared a great wonder in heaven; a woman clothed with the sun, and the moon under her feet, and upon her head a crown of twelve stars: And she being with child cried, travailing in birth, and pained to be delivered."*

5. After the seventh trumpet, what *"great wonder"* did John observe in heaven? (12:1)

6. *"Woman"* (12:1). The immediate and distant context points to the woman as being Israel, and the sun, moon and stars as the family of which the nation came. (Cf. Genesis 37:9, 10; Isaiah 26:17, 18; 66:7 ff.; Micah 4:10; 5:3.) In what sense did Israel bring forth Jesus?

This *"woman"* is vividly described as being clothed with the sun, with the moon underneath her feet, and wearing a crown of twelve stars. These details clearly point back to Joseph's dream in Genesis 37:9–11, which helps us understand their meaning. The sun, then, would symbolize Jacob, the moon represents Rachel (who became a symbol of Jewish motherhood, as she was referenced weeping for her children by the Prophet Jeremiah; Matthew informs us this was fulfilled at the birth of Jesus in Bethlehem, the City of David the King when Herod slaughtered Judah's men-children under two years of age. Rachel's Tomb can be seen in Bethlehem today), and the twelve stars stand for the twelve sons of Jacob, the patriarchs of the Twelve Tribes of Israel. Here, the woman, symbolizing Israel, is seen at a specific point in Israel's history—just before the birth of the Messiah.

7. How did John describe the woman in his vision? (12:2)

In this vision, Israel is depicted as being in the final stages of pregnancy, experiencing the pains of labor and about to give birth (what hardship, pain, and travails had Israel endured, granted, often at her own doing, having swerved aside into idolatry and spiritual immorality as a nation, leading up to Messiah's birth!). At that critical moment, an attempt is made to destroy the child, as described in verses 3–4:

> *"And there appeared another wonder in heaven; and behold a great red dragon, having seven heads and ten horns, and seven crowns upon his heads. And his tail drew the third part of the stars of heaven, and did cast them to the earth: and the dragon stood before the woman which was ready to be delivered, for to devour her child as soon as it was born."*

This dragon, a symbol of Satan, is poised to destroy the Messiah, Jesus, as soon as He is born, illustrating the intense spiritual warfare surrounding His coming into the world.

8. Where does the main action takes place in each section—heaven or earth, or both: Section 1 - Rev. 12:1–4; Section 2 - Rev. 12:7-12; Section 3 - Rev. 12:13-17

9. Which symbol is interpreted by the text?

10. What two kinds of angels are in this vision?

11. Who is the main "actor" in each of the two signs?

Verses 3-4: The Dragon's Fierce Opposition

In verse 3, John describes a great red dragon, which represents Satan in all his ferocity. He is portrayed as having seven heads and ten horns, symbolizing the final form of the Fourth Gentile Empire, now operating under Satan's dominion and authority.

In verse 4, Satan is depicted using his access to earth, descending from his current position in the atmospheric heavens, bringing with him his entire host of fallen angels. The *"third part of the stars"* that Satan draws with his tail represents these fallen angels, as one-third of the angelic host followed Satan in his rebellion. Satan gathers these fallen angels in the Land of Israel with the intent of destroying the Child at His birth. Satan's primary method was to manipulate human governments, for he is the prince of the power of the air and the ruler of this world. He worked through the Roman Empire, particularly using Herod, who ordered the slaughter of the infants in Bethlehem in an attempt to destroy the Messiah.

Throughout the ministry of Jesus, Satan orchestrated numerous efforts to have Him killed—either prematurely or by the wrong means. For the atonement to be accomplished, Jesus had to die not only at the proper time, during the Jewish Passover, but also in the correct manner —by crucifixion. Any attempt to kill Him outside of God's perfect timing or method would have thwarted the plan of redemption. Scripture repeatedly records that these attempts failed, with the declaration: *"His hour was not yet come"* (John 7:30; John 8:20). Verses 3–4 reflect these persistent efforts to destroy the Messiah, emphasizing Satan's determination to disrupt God's redemptive plan by targeting the Child before the appointed time or by the wrong method.

12. Write your impressions of each actor, as suggested by each portrait of symbols:

WOMAN (verses 1, 2):

____

____

DRAGON (verses 3, 4):

____

____

13. What power does the dragon have?

____

____

14. In what activities was the great (e.g., ginormous) red dragon involved? (verse 4)

____

____

15. What is the dragon's objective in the ambush (verse 4)?

____

____

16. *"He might devour her child"* (12:4). The child is Jesus. How did Satan ("*great red dragon*") try to kill Jesus? See Matthew 2:13ff.

____

Verse 5-6: The Birth of Messiah (v. 5) & Israel's Providential Protection (v. 6)

Finally, His hour did come, as described in verse 5:

> *"And she brought forth a man child, who was to rule all nations with a rod of iron: and her child was caught up unto God, and to his throne."*

Jesus died at the appointed time and in the appointed way. Following His resurrection, He ascended to the throne of God, an event that took place at the Mount of Olives. These first five verses provide a concise historical overview of the Messiah's life, spanning from just before His birth to His Ascension. They also summarize the ongoing history of Satan's persecution of the woman, Israel.

17. What important role identifies the male child?

---

18. What did John say about the child born to the woman? (12:5)

---

19. What happened to the newborn child? (12:5)

---

20. How is Genesis 3:15 (known as the "protevangelium," or first evangel) related to this?

---

21. *"Rule all nations"* (12:5). When will Christ do this?

Verse 6 shifts focus to a future persecution:

"And the woman fled into the wilderness, where she hath a place prepared of God, that they should feed her there a thousand two hundred and threescore days."

This verse anticipates events during the middle of the Tribulation. Faced with intense persecution, the woman, symbolizing Israel, will flee to a wilderness location prepared by God. There, she will find refuge and provision for 1,260 days, corresponding to the 3½ years of the second half of the Great Tribulation.

22. Where did the woman go right after giving birth? (12:6)

____

____

23. Why doesn't the dragon succeed in his murder plot?

____

____

24. What references to God do you see in the paragraph?

____

____

II. Satan's Wrath Against Israel Unleashed in the Conflict of the Cosmos — (Rev. 12:7–12)

Verses 7-9: War in Heaven

While verse 6 describes the woman fleeing, it doesn't explain why she is on the run. The second part of this chapter clarifies the reason behind Satan's persecution of Israel. In Satan's third abode, a war will break out between Michael and the elect angels against Satan and his fallen angels. Verse 7 records this conflict:

"And there was war in heaven: Michael and his angels fought against the dragon; and the dragon fought and his angels."

25. Compare the locations mentioned in the first and last lines of verses 7-9.

___

___

26. What was taking place in heaven in John's vision? (12:7)

___

___

27. What is the outcome?

___

___

Ultimately, Michael will triumph in this battle, leading to three significant outcomes described in verses 8–12. The first result is that Satan and his angels will be cast out of the atmospheric heavens, as stated in verses 8–9:

> *"And prevailed not; neither was their place found any more in heaven. And the great dragon was cast out, that old serpent, called the Devil, and Satan, which deceiveth the whole world: he was cast out into the earth, and his angels were cast out with him."*

Satan and his fallen angels will be cast down to the earth, his fourth and final abode where they will remain confined for the second half of the Tribulation, before finally being chained during the Millennial Reign of Christ, loosed for a little season, and subsequently condemned for eternity in the Lake of Fire.

28. By what names was the dragon known? (12:9)

___

___

29. "Old Serpent" (i.e., ancient snake) (12:9). What part of Scripture does this remind you of?

___

___

30. What happened to the dragon and his angels? (12:8–9)

31. What is so ominous about verse 9b?

Verses 10-12: Rejoicing & Woe

The second result of Michael's victory is a time of rejoicing in Heaven, described in verses 10–12a:

> *"And I heard a loud voice saying in heaven, Now is come salvation, and strength, and the kingdom of our God, and the power of his Christ: for the accuser of our brethren is cast down, which accused them before our God day and night. And they overcame him by the blood of the Lamb, and by the word of their testimony; and they loved not their lives unto the death. Therefore rejoice, ye heavens, and ye that dwell in them."*

Satan's access to Heaven will be permanently revoked. No longer will he have the ability to stand before God and accuse the brethren.

32. What did a voice from heaven announce? (12:10)

33. How did the voice from heaven refer to Satan? (12:10)

34. *"Devil … Satan"* (12:9). Devil means *"slanderer,"* and Satan means *"adversary."* Relate these meanings to *"deceives"* (verse 9) and *"accuser"* (verse 10).

---

35. What is the subject of praise (verse 10)?

---

36. Who are "our brethren"?

---

37. What was their experience (verse 11)?

---

38. What is the contrast in verse 12?

---

39. *"They overcame him"* (12:11). What three things brought victory to the martyrs in Satan's attacks?

---

40. How was the blood of the Lamb effective in their deliverance?

The third result, however, is woe for the earth and the sea, as stated in verse 12b:

> *"Woe to the inhabiters of the earth and of the sea! for the devil is come down unto you, having great wrath, because he knoweth that he hath but a short time."*

Once confined to the earth, Satan will know his time is limited to 3½ years. This realization will fuel his intense wrath, making him more dangerous than ever before. While verses 1–6 detail Satan's persecution of Israel historically and prophetically, verses 7–12 reveal the reason behind it: Satan's confinement to the earth will provoke his unrelenting fury against Israel during the Tribulation.

41. What warning was sounded to the earth and sea? Why? (12:12)

____

____

42. *"He hath but a short time"* (12:12). Satan would have only a short time for what?

____

____

43. Compare the devil's permitted powers (verse 12b) with his expulsion (verse 10b).

____

____

44. Who is winning the CONFLICT between God and Satan?

____

____

III. The Enemy's Pursuit of God's People — (Rev. 12:13–17)

These verses detail Satan's persecution of the woman, Israel, during the second half of the Tribulation. Verse 13 ties together the thoughts from verses 6 and 12:

> *"And when the dragon saw that he was cast unto the earth, he persecuted the woman which brought forth the man child."*

45. How does this section expand on the phrase in verse 12, *"having great wrath"*?

Verse 13: Satan's Pursuit of Israel

In verse 6, the woman is fleeing. In verse 12, Satan, having been cast down to the earth, is enraged because he knows his time is short. By verse 13, this fury drives him to actively persecute the woman, Israel. The woman's flight in verse 6 is directly connected to Satan's persecution in verse 13, and his persecution is fueled by his awareness, described in verse 12, that his time is limited. From this point forward, an intense, all-out war against the Jewish people will unfold during the second half of the Tribulation.

46. Recall the reference to 1,260 days in verse 6. How many years is this?

47. How is this represented by the phrase, *"a time and times and half a time"* in the next verse (verse 14)?

Verse 14: Israel's Supernatural Escape

Verse 14 reinforces the message of verse 6, describing the woman fleeing into the wilderness to a place God has prepared for her:

> *"And to the woman were given two wings of a great eagle, that she might fly into the wilderness, into her place, where she is nourished for a time, and times, and half a time, from the face of the serpent."*

In this place of refuge, the woman, representing Israel, will be protected and sustained for 3½ years—the second half of the Tribulation. According to Micah 2:12–13, this wilderness refuge is Bozrah, known in Greek as Petra:

> *"I will surely assemble, O Jacob, all of thee; I will surely gather the remnant of Israel; I will put them together as the sheep of Bozrah, as the flock in the midst of their fold: they shall make great noise by reason of the multitude of men.*

The breaker is come up before them: they have broken up, and have passed through the gate, and are gone out by it: and their king shall pass before them, and the LORD on the head of them."

48. "*Two wings … that she might fly*" (12:14). Do you think these are symbolical references, or literal? If the former, what is symbolized?

____

____

These prophetic insights from Micah show us that, contrary to what many assume about the Second Advent, Jesus Christ is not coming straight from the clouds to the Mount of Olives (and rest assured, what Micah envisioned in no way needs to be seen as contradicting what the angels told the Apostles of our Lord at the Ascension of Christ as recorded by Luke in Acts 1:11), but He will return to the Mount of Olives having come from Bozrah, leading His people (both the Remnant of Israel on earth at Petra, as well as those who will be behind Him on white horses (cf., Rev. 19:11ff) to ascend the Mount of Olives, which will then subsequently split beneath His feet as foretold by Zechariah.

Compare Isaiah 63:1-3

"Who is this that cometh from Edom, with dyed garments from Bozrah? this that is glorious in his apparel, travelling in the greatness of his strength? I that speak in righteousness, mighty to save. Wherefore art thou red in thine apparel, and thy garments like him that treadeth in the winefat? I have trodden the winepress alone; and of the people there was none with me: for I will tread them in mine anger, and trample them in my fury; and their blood shall be sprinkled upon my garments, and I will stain all my raiment."

Compare also Zechariah 14:4

"And his feet shall stand in that day upon the mount of Olives, which is before Jerusalem on the east, and the mount of Olives shall cleave in the midst thereof toward the east and toward the west, and there shall be a very great valley; and half of the mountain shall remove toward the north, and half of it toward the south."

Verse 15: The Dragon's Flood of Fury

The method Satan will use to persecute the Jews is described in verse 15:

> *"And the serpent cast out of his mouth water as a flood after the woman, that he might cause her to be carried away of the flood."*

49. How does Satan try to destroy the woman?

This verse depicts Satan spewing water like a flood, symbolizing a military invasion. In Scripture, the figure of a flood, when used symbolically, consistently represents military action. Thus, the persecution will take the form of a military invasion that leads to the collapse of the State of Israel midway through the Tribulation. Although the purpose of this invasion will be to annihilate the Jewish people, it will ultimately fail.

Verse 16: Earth's Divine Intervention

The reason this attempt will fail is revealed in verse 16:

> *"And the earth helped the woman, and the earth opened her mouth, and swallowed up the flood which the dragon cast out of his mouth."*

50. What help does the woman have?

The earth opening up to swallow the flood symbolizes divine intervention, a method God often used in the Old Testament to deliver His people (cf. Numbers 16:30–33, Exodus 15:12, and Psalm 106:17). In the same way, God will intervene, preventing the destruction of the Jews in the middle of the Tribulation. This attempt to wipe them out will not succeed.

51. Is God explicitly mentioned in this connection (verse 13–16)?

Verse 17: The Dragon's War with the Faithful

As a result, Satan will launch a long-term campaign to destroy the Jewish people, as described in verse 17:

> *"And the dragon was wroth with the woman, and went to make war with the remnant of her seed, which keep the commandments of God, and have the testimony of Jesus Christ."*

His war will target two specific groups of Jews: first, those who keep the commandments of God, referring to Orthodox Jews; and second, those who have the testimony of Jesus, which includes the believing Jewish remnant of the Tribulation as well as, despite the Watchtower's false teachings, the 144,000 Jewish evangelists mentioned earlier in Revelation 7.

52. What does Satan do when he fails to destroy the woman (verse 17)?

---

53. What observations do you have from the following related verses? Exodus 19:4; Deuteronomy 32:11, 12; Isaiah 59:19; Luke 14:26; John 12:25; John 12:31–33; John 15:20; Colossians 1:13, 14

---

54. What can we learn about Satan (his character, activities, and destiny) from this passage?

---

55. In what way does Satan try to oppose God today?

---

56. What do we learn about God from this passage?

____

____

57. What does this passage tell us about God's people?

____

____

58. In what ways does Satan try to tempt and hurt us?

____

____

59. How can we strengthen ourselves against Satan's attempts to weaken and tempt us?

____

____

60. What can you do this week to strengthen your hold on the testimony of Jesus?

____

____

Conclusion

So then, in our studies of these *Four Women of the Apocalypse*, the second woman represents Israel, who will face persecution from Satan. Revelation 13 reveals the two individuals Satan will use to carry out this persecution: the Antichrist and the False Prophet.

CHAPTER THREE

The Great Harlot

Introduction

This third woman represents Ecclesiastical Babylon, the one-world religious system that will dominate during the Great Tribulation. We can break this chapter down into six sections: first, the portrait of the harlot; second, the harlot's crime; third, the harlot's global power system; fourth, the meaning of the term *"many waters"*; fifth, the final and providential destruction of the harlot; and last, the end of the earthly dominion of the harlot. The Apostle John received an invitation to witness the harlot in verse 1:

> *"And there came one of the seven angels that had the seven vials, and talked with me, saying unto me, Come hither; I will shew unto thee the judgment of the great whore that sitteth upon many waters."*

1. How do the first two lines relate this segment to the preceding passage?

____

____

> *"GREAT"*: The sense of great is to be understood by the things it is intended to qualify. Great pain or wrath is violent pain or wrath; great love is ardent love; great peace is entire peace; a great name is

> extensive renown; a great evil or sin, is a sin of deep malignity, &c. [e.g., Malignity refers to deep-rooted hatred or malice, often without cause, and the extreme evil or destructive nature of something, such as sin or a disease. It conveys intense spite and malevolence. In the context of this passage and broader Scripture, the ultimate object of this hatred is God, and His Christ, thereby, His people, called by His name, by way of association]. *"WHORE"*: In Scripture, idolatry ; the desertion of the worship of the true God, for the worship of idols. Prophets.
>
> ~ Noah Webster, 1828

2. What are some examples of champions or winners?

____

____

3. If your life was being threatened and you could hire anyone in the world to be your personal bodyguard, whom would you pick?

____

____

4. What do you think of when you hear someone talk of a "new world order"?

____

____

I. A Portrait of Deception: The Great Harlot's Description — Revelation 17:1–5

This harlot represents the counterfeit bride of the Messiah. She is a religious prostitute, in stark contrast to the pure virgin—the true Bride of Christ. This is the final manifestation of the Jezebel system that began to manifest itself in the first few centuries of the early church that led to many of the doctrinal persuasions that we see within Roman Catholicism (Rev. 2:20–22) and other deviant doctrinal systems throughout the broad spectrum of "Christendom." Many have erred from the faith that was *"once delivered"* unto the saints, and have swerved away from the Bible as the sole authority for all matters of faith and practice.

Verse 1: The Invitation to Witness the Harlot's Judgment

> The harlot of verse 1 is the woman of verse 3. The woman is "the great city" (verse 18), which is Babylon (verse 5). This is the first clue that much of this passage is to be interpreted figuratively. References to Babylon may be to a real city, but also, and more importantly, to a world system, i.e., religious, political and commercial. As you study about Babylon in these passages, think world system or world empire.
>
> ~ Irving L. Jensen

To prostitute something, in its verb form, means to take something that has a legitimate purpose and use it in a sinful or improper way. Just as a harlot misuses the God-given sexual act, which is intended for a proper use within marriage (Heb. 13:4), so too, false religious systems misuse what was meant for pure and unadulterated worship of the one true God of the Bible. In Scripture, any false religion is likened to spiritual fornication or prostitution (cf., Hos. 1–2; Jer. 2:20; 3:1–9; Ezek. 16:15–41; 23:5–44). This religious *"whore"* (to use John's terminology from the King's Jacobean English, this is an adult Bible study, so keep your big boy pants on, so as not to detract from the FORCE of the Revelator's words, it means exactly what it says, and it says exactly what it means, when we define it the way John did) stands in stark opposition to the Bride of the Messiah, falsely using religion. True religion is defined in James 1:26–27, but this harlot represents false religion. Additionally, she is described as sitting on many waters, which represent peoples and nations (v. 15), signifying that she will hold religious sway over a multitude of nations.

5. Are the quoted words of verses 1b and 2 a vision or an announcement to John about a vision he would see?

---

6. If the latter, where in the segment does the vision begin?

---

7. "*Sitteth upon many waters*" (17:1). Verse 15 interprets this symbol. How does this support the view that Babylon here is a world system, not just a city?

Verses 2–3: The Harlot's Influence and Alignment with the Beast

Moreover, she will receive the backing of the civil government, as seen in verses 2–3:

> *"With whom the kings of the earth have committed fornication, and the inhabitants of the earth have been made drunk with the wine of her fornication. So he carried me away in the spirit into the wilderness: and I saw a woman sit upon a scarlet coloured beast, full of names of blasphemy, having seven heads and ten horns."*

In verse 2, we see that the harlot will have the backing of civil government during the first half of the Tribulation. This will mark the height of the unholy union of church and state. In verse 3, she is pictured as sitting upon a scarlet-colored beast with seven heads and ten horns. This beast represents the governmental system during the first half of the Great Tribulation, indicating that the harlot exercises her power with the support of the civil authorities.

8. "*Fornication*" (17:2). What is Babylon's moral condition, according to this and other references of the segment?

---

9. "*Scarlet coloured beast*" (17:3). See 13:1. This is the sea beast, known especially for his blasphemies against God (13:5, 6). What does this reveal about Babylon as a religious system?

10. What else is revealed about this by verse 6a?

11. *"Seven heads and ten horns"* (17:3). These symbols are interpreted by 17:9, 10 and 12. What does this reveal about Babylon's political power?

Verses 4–5: The Harlot's External Beauty and Internal Corruption

John further identifies the harlot in verses 4–5:

> *"And the woman was arrayed in purple and scarlet colour, and decked with gold and precious stones and pearls, having a golden cup in her hand full of abominations and filthiness of her fornication: And upon her forehead was a name written, MYSTERY, BABYLON THE GREAT, THE MOTHER OF HARLOTS AND ABOMINATIONS OF THE EARTH."*

12. What is the impact of "great"?

13. What sin does this paragraph identify? Note: keep in mind the difference between harlotry and adultery. The former is fornication of a prostitute; adultery is sexual unfaithfulness of a husband or wife.

14. With what two groups does the harlot sin?

In verse 4, the harlot is depicted as both wealthy and influential. She is also guilty of spiritual fornication, holding in her hand a golden cup filled with abominations and the unclean things of her fornication. This woman symbolizes Ecclesiastical Babylon, the ecumenical one-world religious system that will dominate the religious landscape during the first half of the Great Tribulation. In verse 5, she is given the title:

> *"MYSTERY, BABYLON THE GREAT, THE MOTHER OF HARLOTS AND ABOMINATIONS OF THE EARTH."*

This marks the final form of the apostate church, a process that has unfolded over these last two millennia since Christ ascended. Some examples in more recent history include the early 1900s here in the United States, where certain movements began to significantly deviate from biblical truth, as documented in the rise of the modernist movement within Protestantism, which embraced liberal theology. This movement sought to reconcile Christian teachings with modern scientific thought and the social changes of the time. One of the more notable examples was the formation of the Federal Council of Churches in 1908, which promoted a more ecumenical approach and downplayed doctrinal distinctives in favor of social and political engagement. This often involved a denial of key doctrines such as the virgin birth, the deity of Christ, and the authority of Scripture. These theological shifts represent just one instance of the broader trend of doctrinal compromise that has occurred at various points in church history, ultimately leading to the apostasy prophesied in Scripture. We could spend hours discussing all the variant factions that have promulgated a false religion, a false Christ, and a false gospel.

15. Immorality is the first description of Babylon given in this section of Revelation, a priority that suggests prominence. In the tribulation period moral corruption will be at its worst. To what extent is this a growing trend in the world today?

16. What systems (i.e., "*Babylon*") in the world today are hostile to God?

In verse 5, the woman is called the *"Mother of Harlots,"* exposing the reality for John's readership that Ecclesiastical Babylon would not only be guilty of spiritual adultery herself (*"and when lust hath conceived, it bringeth forth sin . . ."*) but would also become the bitter well-spring and source of widespread corruption. Just as a mother's children often follow in her footsteps, this false religious system will mature (*"and sin when it is finished . . ."*) and spread idolatry and rebellion, drawing others with her seductive clutches (Prov. 5-7) into the same sinful practices. Her title sheds light on the generational nature of her corruption, as she will be guilty of leading many nations and many people into spiritual fornication. Ultimately, she is the sinful root of bitterness that feeds a vast network of false religions, perhaps like an Aspen system of groves here in the Rockies, all heading toward the tinderbox of God's impending judgment (*"it bringeth forth death"*).

Today, the broader "Christian" world (using the term loosely) oftentimes appears drunk, disorderly, and deaf (likely due to some of her choice in musical entertainment, among other things) to the dangers of ecumenicism and the religious STD's that come from getting in bed with every other thing that paints itself up to look like the *"Bride,"* when in fact, often just a cursory glance at a doctrinal statement (if you can find one) would reveal that these are merely a "harlot" in disguise painted all up and decked with ornaments to try and woo the simple to turn aside from the truth. Don't get mad at me. I'm simply reading and studying the Bible in light of the signs of the times around us. Be careful who you get in bed with spiritually. By that, I mean, take care who you walk with intimately in your pursuit of doctrine. Doctrine is the teaching that unites us, but the practice that divides us. It is important to maintain both personal and ecclesiastical (corporate) separation from that which would defile. Now, this doesn't mean that you cannot interact with others in the community. It means, don't just let anybody in to the intimate places of your faith. Community development calls on us to let our light shine, and for others to see our good works, and glorify our Father in heaven. Community impact means that we, as a church, must engage outside of these four walls, which means also that sometimes those outside these walls will make their way in, where we can teach them, but the core of the church family must remain united in one faith, one Lord, one baptism, and earnestly contend for the faith once delivered unto the saints. Let's not allow the seeds of ecumenism to be spread in the garden bed of the family of God, but let's do strive to overcome evil with good, and stay close to the vine, so we can bring forth much fruit.

17. What should be the reactions and actions of Christians and the church?

____

____

18. What are your observations on these related verses: Genesis 10:10; 11:9; Isaiah 13:19, 20; Jeremiah 50; 51; Psalm 2:1–3; 83:1–8.

____

____

II. Her Crimes Against the Saints — (Rev. 17:6)

"And I saw the woman drunken with the blood of the saints, and with the blood of the martyrs of Jesus: And when I saw her, I wondered with great admiration."

Her crime is one of persecution, as she will seek to punish all who refuse to join her in her spiritual adulteries. Believers living during that time who reject this one-world religious system will face severe persecution from it.

19. Who is the first person John sees in the vision?

____

____

20. What could John tell about the woman he saw? (17:6)

____

____

21. What amazed John? (17:6)

____

____

22. How is she identified in verse 18?

____

____

23. What other awful sin is the woman guilty of (verse 6a)?

____

____

24. What are your observations on these other related verses: Isaiah 1:21; 23:16 ff.; Jeremiah 2:20; 3:1, 6–10; Ezekiel 16:30–43; Nahum 3:4; Revelation 12:3; Revelation 16:12–16.

____

____

III. Her Connection to the Global Power System — (Rev. 17:7–14)

"And the angel said unto me, Wherefore didst thou marvel? I will tell thee the mystery of the woman, and of the beast that carrieth her, which hath the seven heads and ten horns. The beast that thou sawest was, and is not; and shall ascend out of the bottomless pit, and go into perdition: and they that dwell on the earth shall wonder, whose names were not written in the book of life from the foundation of the world, when they behold the beast that was, and is not, and yet is. And here is the mind which hath wisdom. The seven heads are seven mountains, on which the woman sitteth. And there are seven kings: five are fallen, and one is, and the other is not yet come; and when he cometh, he must continue a short space. And the beast that was, and is not, even he is the eighth, and is of the seven, and goeth into perdition. And the ten horns which thou sawest are ten kings, which have received no kingdom as yet; but receive power as kings one hour with the beast. These have one mind, and shall give their power and strength unto the beast. These shall make war with the

Lamb, and the Lamb shall overcome them: for he is Lord of lords, and King of kings: and they that are with him are called, and chosen, and faithful."

25. How did the angel react to John's astonishment? (17:7)

____

____

26. What does the beast have (verse 7b)?

____

____

27. Why does the angel explain the mystery of the woman and the beast?

____

____

28. Where in the passage does the angel prophesy that the woman will be consumed?

____

____

29. Do any of these appear in the vision: God, Christ, saints? If so, where?

____

____

30. What three time verbs refer to the beast's rule (verse 8)?

____

____

31. How are unbelievers identified here (verse 8b)?

____

____

32. What causes them to wonder?

This passage describes the governmental system that will back Ecclesiastical Babylon during the first half of the Tribulation. In short, this system will consist of ten kings (*"horns"*) ruling over ten kingdoms. In the middle of the Tribulation, all the kings will give their authority to the Antichrist, who will then rule the world until the end of the Tribulation, culminating in the Second Coming of the Messiah.

33. Who are the seven heads? (vv. 9-11)

---

34. What is the eventual fate of the last of them?

---

35. Compare this with the eventual fate of the beast.

---

36. What do people need in light of the events that are coming? (17:9)

---

37. "Ten horns" (17:12). This is a league of ten nations which align with the beast to destroy the harlot, Babylon (verses 16, 17). Who originates this plan to destroy Babylon (verse 17)?

---

38. What action will the ten kings take and what will be the result? (17:13–14)

IV. The Metaphor of 'Many Waters' — (Rev. 17:15)

"And he saith unto me, The waters which thou sawest, where the whore sitteth, are peoples, and multitudes, and nations, and tongues."

The term *"many waters"* upon which the woman sits represents humanity, the vast population of the world. This illustrates that Ecclesiastical Babylon will exercise control over the religious affairs of the entire world during the first half of the Tribulation.

39. What do the *"many waters"* symbolize in Revelation 17:15, and how does this help us understand the scope and breadth of Ecclesiastical Babylon's influence?

40. In what ways might Ecclesiastical Babylon attempt to exercise control over the religious affairs of the world during the Tribulation?

V. Her Final Destruction by Divine Design — (Rev. 17:16–17)

"And the ten horns which thou sawest upon the beast, these shall hate the whore, and shall make her desolate and naked, and shall eat her flesh, and burn her with fire. For God hath put in their hearts to fulfil his will, and to agree, and give their kingdom unto the beast, until the words of God shall be fulfilled."

This passage describes the destruction of Ecclesiastical Babylon that will take place in the middle of the Tribulation. She will be destroyed by the ten horns, the kings ruling at that time, and by the beast, who is the Antichrist. While this religious system has the support of government during the first half of the Tribulation, at the middle point, the Antichrist and his ten allies will destroy this one-world religious system. This paves the way for the Antichrist to become both the one-world religious ruler and the one-world political ruler.

41. To whom do the ten kings give their federated kingdom?

42. What do they and the beast do? How thorough is the harlot's destruction?

43. How is this a part of God's sovereign will?

44. Why do you think idolatry (worship of false gods) is described as adultery in the Bible?

VI. Her Earthly Dominion and Its End — (Rev. 17:18)

"And the woman which thou sawest is that great city, which reigneth over the kings of the earth."

This woman also represents a city, specifically the city where this religious system will be centered. Taken literally, this refers to the rebuilt city of Babylon during the Great Tribulation.

45. How significant do you think it is that ancient Babylon is being rebuilt in modern-day Iraq?

46. Why does the angel's explanation conclude with verse 18?

____

____

47. From a human standpoint, why would the beast want to wipe out Babylon? In answering this, keep in mind that the woman (Babylon) *"reigneth over the kings of the earth"* (17:18).

____

____

48. What are some of the bright, positive notes of this passage? Apply them to your own life. For example, how does it affect your everyday living to know that the overcoming Lamb is your Savior and the sovereign God is your Lord? If you are studying with a group, why not devote testimony time to this uplifting theme?

____

____

49. How do you think you should respond differently to worldly events and situations after having studied this chapter?

____

____

50. In what ways do you need to reaffirm your commitment, devotion, and loyalty to Jesus Christ this week?

____

____

51. What difference does it make that Jesus is the Lord of lords and King of kings?

____

____

52. How should our behavior or life-style reflect the truth that Jesus is Lord of

lords and King of kings?

____

____

53. In what areas of your life do you need more of God's wisdom?

____

____

54. What can you use to remind yourself each day this week of God's rule and superiority over all evil in the world?

____

____

55. What can you do to learn from the wisdom of more mature Christians?

____

____

CHAPTER FOUR

The Bride & Wife of Messiah

Introduction

"For I am jealous over you with godly jealousy: for I have espoused you to one husband, that I may present you as a chaste virgin to Christ."

2 Corinthians 11:2

The fourth woman is the Bride and Wife of the Messiah, portrayed in Revelation 19:6–9. Many years ago, Dr. C. I. Scofield penned a brief but significant work entitled, Rightly Dividing the Word of Truth. In it, he emphasized that a sound grasp of Scripture depends upon maintaining the proper distinctions found therein. Indeed, whether one is Dispensational or not often hinges on the recognition of these vital biblical distinctions. When they go unrecognized, the Scriptures can appear contradictory.

For instance, as Dr. Arnold Fruchtenbaum has rightly observed, from Adam to Noah, humanity's diet was strictly vegetarian. From Noah to Moses, God permitted mankind to eat anything without restriction. From Moses until the earthly ministry of Jesus the Messiah, only certain meats were allowed—such as beef—while others, like shrimp or ham, were prohibited. Since the time of Christ, however, all meats have once again been declared "clean," and the believer is free to eat whatever he desires, provided it is received with thanksgiving.

If we fail to acknowledge these chronological distinctions—how

God has dealt with humanity in different ways at different times—we might conclude that God is contradicting Himself. After all, one passage says *"thou mayest,"* and another seems to say *"thou shalt not"* concerning the very same subject.

One of the most essential biblical distinctions is that which exists between Israel and the Church. Failing to maintain this distinction will inevitably lead to misinterpretation. Scripture consistently differentiates between Israel and the Church in several ways, one of which is the contrast between "the Wife" and "the Bride." The Word of God portrays Israel as the "Wife of Jehovah," whereas the Church is shown to be "the Bride of Christ (Messiah)." In the pages that follow, we will examine what the Scriptures teach about these two relationships and see how these distinctions are upheld.

I. ISRAEL AS THE WIFE OF JEHOVAH — (VARIOUS SCRIPTURES)

The Scriptures portray Israel as the Wife of Jehovah through various perspectives and dimensions. This covenant bond may be understood in six distinct stages of progression. Four of these stages have already transpired within history, and we now live in the fifth stage of the relationship between Israel and the Church. The sixth stage still lies ahead.

A. The Initial Covenant (Marriage)

To the casual observer, the Book of Deuteronomy might seem like little more than a restatement of matters already covered in Exodus, Leviticus, and Numbers. Indeed, the very name "Deuteronomy" signifies "second law" or, rather, "a repetition of the Law." While much of its content parallels what we have in the first three books of Moses, Deuteronomy is far from a mere repetition. The entire structure of this book reflects both an ancient treaty format and an ancient marriage contract. In essence, Moses took the various components found in Exodus, Leviticus, and Numbers and presented them as a marriage covenant—an agreement between Israel and God by which Israel becomes the Wife of Jehovah.

Deuteronomy is extensive, and it is not feasible here to show how the entire book functions in this contractual framework. Instead, we will focus on several key passages, beginning with Deuteronomy 5:1–3.

There we see God's covenant with Israel at Mount Sinai, which the prophets later view as a marriage contract.

1. Before any specific word is spoken in this section about what Israel must do, Moses speaks of what God has done for Israel. In 4:44–49 and 5:6, what specific acts of God are called to mind, and how would this background encourage Israel to keep God's commands?

____

____

2. What did Moses say about the law to the Israelites? (5:1–4)

____

____

Next, Deuteronomy 6:10–15 highlights God's jealousy on behalf of His Wife, Israel, warning her not to stray into adultery by following other gods. The very reason given is the Lord's protective love for His people, a love that would—even in discipline—remove Israel from the Land if she proved unfaithful.

3. What was Israel told to remember when the Lord brings them into the land? (6:10–12)

____

____

4. How was Israel commanded to fear God? (6:13)

____

____

5. What is the consequence for following other gods? (6:14–15)

____

____

6. Moses exhorts Israel not to test the Lord as they did at Massah (v. 16). At that time, Israel was deep in the wilderness, lacking water, and on the verge of death. They tested God by doubting his care for them (Ex. 17:1–7). How is the

test Israel will face in the land different from the one they faced in the wilderness? How is it similar? (See especially vv. 10–15; compare Prov. 30:8–9.)

____

____

7. For Israel, "forgetting" in this passage is more than amnesia; it is willfully embracing their pride and the lies they tell themselves in their hearts. What are the specific lies Israel will be tempted to speak to themselves? How does Moses rebuke those lies?

____

____

In Deuteronomy 7:6–11, we find the reaffirmation of Israel's chosen status. God did not select Israel for her size or power. Rather, He loved her and so entered into a covenant relationship spelled out here in Deuteronomy. With that privilege comes responsibility, as He urges Israel to be faithful, loyal, and obedient to Him.

8. What *"gods"* are worshiped in our culture today?

____

____

9. How do some people worship things without even realizing it?

____

____

10. How is Israel the treasured possession of God? (7:6)

____

____

11. What was the motive of God to choose Israel over other nations? (7:7–8)

____

____

12. How faithful is God? (7:9–10)

____

____

13. To what was Israel told to pay special attention? (7:11–12)

____

____

14. How do impersonal idols ruin a personal relationship with God?

____

____

15. What is an idol you need to forsake in order to follow God faithfully?

____

____

As noted earlier, the prophets consistently portray this covenant as a marriage bond. One example is in Ezekiel 16:8, which describes Israel's wedding night with Jehovah, signifying the covenant established at Sinai.

Thus, the first phase in Israel's role as the Wife of Jehovah is the marital agreement recorded throughout Deuteronomy. In this sacred text, we see a strong unity of law and love—an entire book serving as the foundation for Israel's covenant, wherein she becomes bound to her divine Husband.

B. The Great Unfaithfulness (Adultery)

Although Israel was repeatedly counseled to remain faithful to her divine Husband, she instead engaged in a grievous act of adultery, as testified by several of the Old Testament prophets. Jeremiah 3:1–5 describes how Israel, rather than committing a single instance of unfaithfulness, played the harlot with numerous lovers. Jeremiah 3:20 likens her to a wife who treacherously turns away from her husband. Because of this persistent adulterous behavior, Jeremiah 31:32 declares that the original marriage covenant was broken—not through any fault of God, for He remained a faithful Husband, but through Israel's pursuit of other gods.

16. What is one of the more outrageous excuses or rationalizations you've heard recently?

____

____

17. What behavior on the part of Israel made it unthinkable that God would return to her? (3:1–3)

____

____

18. How did Judah's talk contrast with her behavior? (3:4–5)

____

____

19. What should a history lesson on God's dealings with His people inspire in us?

____

____

20. How is it possible for people to have no awe of God?

____

____

21. What was ironic about the way Judah cried out to God, or even blamed God, when they were in trouble?

____

____

Ezekiel 16:15–34 presents an extensive account of this infidelity. Israel not only lavished the blessings God had given her upon foreign gods, but also sacrificed her own children in the process. Instead of seeking shelter in her Husband, Jehovah, she turned to the very nations that caused her suffering. Hosea 2:2–5 likewise depicts Israel's harlotry, condemning her for producing children out of this adulterous union.

22. Ezekiel now relates two parables demonstrating that Israel's judgment is well deserved. Israel has long been described as God's vine (see Ps. 80:8ff.; Isa. 5:1ff.) What is it about the vine that makes its burning appropriate? What does this say about the inhabitants of Jerusalem (see Rom. 9:21–24)?

____

____

23. The second parable, one of the most famous in the whole Bible, describes the history of Israel in terms of a foundling that God rescues, nurtures, and eventually marries, raising her to the status of a beautiful queen (16:1–14). How does the queen repay her husband's generosity and love (see vv. 15–34)? Who are Israel's "lovers"? What does Israel's "whoredom" tell us about the nature of idolatry? What other forms does Israel's unfaithfulness take (see vv. 20–21, 23–29)?

____

____

Thus, despite receiving manifold blessings and a great deliverance at God's hand, Israel forsook her Redeemer. By chasing after false deities and alliances, she fell into great adultery and nullified the covenant she once held so dear.

C. The Period of Estrangement (Separation)

Due to Israel's unfaithfulness, a period of separation between God and His people occurred during the time of Isaiah. Isaiah 50:1 acknowledges this rift, noting that many in Israel presumed God had issued them a bill of divorcement. Yet according to Deuteronomy 24:1, a husband had to provide a written bill (i.e., decree) of divorce to finalize such an act. In the days of Isaiah, no written decree existed; thus, the separation could not yet be called a divorce.

24. What sorts of evidence did God challenge Israel to produce to prove that He was the cause of their defeat and captivity? (50:1)

____

25. What are some of the indications of God's tenderness in this prophecy of Isaiah?

26. What specific benefit can we find in the words of Jesus, the Messiah?

27. How is God's Servant, the Messiah, significantly different from the rest of humankind in His responsiveness to God?

28. What is unique in your mind about the concept of a suffering Messiah?

29. Even when He rebukes us, what will God do for us if we ask Him?

This estrangement, lasting roughly a century, came about because of Israel's sins and her continued pursuit of false gods. By removing His blessings—promised in Deuteronomy for covenant faithfulness—God allowed the nation to feel the weight of their unfaithfulness. Yet, throughout this separation, they remained officially undivorced, their covenant bond not wholly dissolved. Consequently, Isaiah's ministry reveals that God and Israel were not divorced at this juncture, but were living under the consequences of a protracted separation.

D. The Formal Break (Divorce)

Despite a century of separation from God, during which the

promised blessings of Deuteronomy remained withheld, Israel still refused to repent and return to her Husband. As a result, the Lord was finally compelled to deliver a bill of divorcement. Jeremiah 3:6–10 captures this moment: it declares Israel's persistent infidelity and reveals that God officially ended the covenant on grounds of her continued adultery. Indeed, one could view the larger context of Jeremiah's prophecy as the entire decree of divorce.

30. Why is it often difficult for us to admit that we're wrong?

____

____

31. What did God tell Jeremiah that Israel had done, with Judah looking on? (3:6–7)

____

____

32. Despite witnessing God's "divorcing" Israel, what did Judah go ahead and do? (3:8–9)

____

____

33. What was the nature of Judah's "return" to God? (3:10)

____

____

Ultimately, in Jeremiah's day, God divorced Israel. The prolonged separation of a hundred years had not brought about genuine repentance, leaving no alternative but to issue the formal bill of divorcement.

E. The Season of Judgment (Punishment)

The original marriage contract in Deuteronomy made it clear that unfaithfulness on Israel's part would inevitably bring God's judgment. After He issued the bill of divorcement, a prolonged season of divine punishment followed. Various prophets testify to this judgment.

Ezekiel 16:35–43 recounts how Israel's former 'lovers'—the same nations whose gods she had pursued—would become her agents of destruction, exacting judgment on God's behalf. This punishment aimed not merely at retribution, but rather at compelling Israel to abandon her sinful ways. Ezekiel later explains in Ezekiel 16:58–59 that this discipline arose because Israel violated the marriage covenant.

34. What punishment does God detail for Jerusalem's unfaithfulness? (16:35–43)

____

____

35. What do you think is the greatest condemnation in the parable of the woman?

____

____

36. In what ways is idolatry portrayed in the parable of the woman?

____

____

37. How do you imagine it felt to Jews to be compared unfavorably to Sodom?

____

____

38. How can we be certain that God will carry through on His words?

____

____

Hosea 2:6–13 further details God's program of punishment. Through divine intervention symbolized by *"thorns"* and a *"wall,"* He would thwart Israel's efforts to return to her false gods, ultimately revealing her desperate need for her true Husband. The material blessings she once misused for idol worship would be stripped away, leaving her to confront her spiritual nakedness.

39. What qualities do you cherish about the person who loves you most?

____

____

40. How did Hosea feel about Gomer? (2:2–13)

____

____

41. What did God say to Israel through Hosea's words? (2:2–13)

____

____

42. What do you expect from God when you "betray" Him repeatedly?

____

____

43. How do you tend to deal with a loved one who has wronged you in some way?

____

____

44. How is God's faithfulness to us an example of the way we should treat others?

____

____

45. What are the "idols" in your life from which you should turn away?

____

____

46. What bruised or broken family relationship of yours needs the healing touch of the Lord?

47. What does this passage say to you about the consequences of sin?

48. In what ways do you think people's attitudes toward morality have changed over the past ten years?

Nevertheless, the Lord consistently calls His people to repent during this period of chastisement. Jeremiah 3:11–18 describes God's plea for Israel's return and promises a future restoration to those who respond. Declaring Himself a Husband to Israel, God assures her of eventual blessings and provision, should she forsake her idolatrous ways and return to Him.

Even now, Israel remains in this phase of punishment—a condition evidenced by ongoing sufferings, global dispersions, and persecutions. Yet the Scriptures attest that one final stage in Israel's relationship with Jehovah still awaits its fulfillment.

F. The Future Restoration (Remarriage and Renewed Blessings)

The writings of the Hebrew prophets do not leave Israel in a hopeless condition; rather, they point to a future day when she will again be the restored Wife of Jehovah. This necessitates a new marriage contract, which is outlined in Jeremiah 31:31–34. Commonly known as the New Covenant, this agreement in many ways serves as a fresh marriage covenant made with both the houses of Israel and Judah. It becomes necessary because the original covenant was broken through Israel's adultery, yet through this new contract she will be restored to a position of blessing.

49. Jeremiah 31:31–34 describes the New Covenant God promises to make with his people. What are the various elements of this New Covenant?

____

____

50. In what ways will the New Covenant be different from the old one?

____

____

Ezekiel 16:60–63 likewise references a future and everlasting covenant—identical to that which Jeremiah describes. Both prophets reveal that this everlasting covenant functions as a renewed marriage agreement, paving the way for Israel's ultimate remarriage to Jehovah.

51. The chapter ends on an unexpected note of hope, as God remembers the covenant Israel broke and determines to make a New Covenant (vv. 59–63). Why does he do this? What is the role of Israel's shame now, and how does God redeem it for his glory?

____

____

Isaiah 54:1–8 further depicts Israel's restoration. There, we learn she will once again bear legitimate children (after having produced many illegitimate ones in her former adulteries), prompting the expansion of her dwelling place. Past unfaithfulness will be forgotten, and Jehovah will renew His role as Husband. He will court Israel as He did when she was young, replacing any temporary forsaking with enduring blessings.

52. What great misfortune for women of Isaiah's day did he compare with Israel's desolation? (54:1)

____

____

53. What did Isaiah predict for Israel in terms of numbers and prosperity? (54:2–3)

____

____

54. What did God promise concerning the shame that Israel brought on

herself? (54:4)

55. What human relationship did Isaiah compare to the relationship between God and His chosen people? (54:5)

56. What comparison did God use to express His treatment of Israel? (54:6–8)

57. What was the duration of God's displeasure relative to His compassion? (54:8)

58. Although Israel brought shame on herself, what did God propose to do about it?

Isaiah 62:4–5 continues this theme by declaring the land—lost due to past infidelity—will be restored, and God will rejoice over His Bride as a bridegroom delights in his new wife.

59. How did Isaiah predict that a change of name would reflect a change of status for Israel? (62:4)

60. What status and emotions went along with marriage for a young woman of Isaiah's time? (62:5)

61. What does it mean to watch for the coming of Christ?

62. What does it mean to "prepare the way of the Lord"?

Hosea 2:14–23 also speaks of Israel's reconciliation. She will be led into the wilderness once more, where the Lord will woo her and give back the vineyards she once possessed. This renewed union brings four results: first, Israel will address God as *"my man"* (Ishi) rather than *"my master"* (Baali), thus eliminating all reminders of false gods. Second, she will enjoy lasting peace and security. Third, she will experience a new betrothal marked by righteousness, justice, lovingkindness, mercies, and faithfulness. Finally, the meaning of Jezreel will shift from *"God scatters"* to *"God sows,"* picturing the restoration of fertility and blessing.

63. What did the Lord plan to do to win Israel back to himself? (2:14–15)

64. By what name would renewed Israel acknowledge her Lord? (2:16)

65. What would God prohibit? (2:17)

66. What would accompany Israel's return to the land? (2:18)

67. What would mark the new relationship between the Lord and Israel? (2:19–23)

In summary, these passages outline six stages in Israel's role as the Wife of Jehovah: the marriage, the great adultery, the separation, the divorce, the period of punishment, and the future remarriage. Though Israel is presently still under punishment for her unfaithfulness, the prophets promise that she will ultimately be reunited with her Husband and enjoy all the blessings of this renewed covenant.

II. THE CHURCH AS THE BRIDE OF THE MESSIAH — REVELATION 19:6–9; 21:9–22:5

In contrast to Israel as the Wife of Jehovah, the Scriptures present a distinctly different picture for the Church in her relationship to the Messiah. Recognizing this contrast is vital for a proper understanding of these two biblical truths.

When we speak of the Church as the Bride of Christ, we mean the entire Body of true believers—past, present, and future—joined together by faith in the Lord Jesus. This collective assembly extends beyond any particular region or denomination. In contrast, a local church refers to those believers gathering in a specific area for worship, edification, and service. While each local congregation is Scripturally autonomous, the Bride is not limited to one location or group; rather, she encompasses all who truly belong to the Lord.

According to the New Testament, the Church is presently betrothed to the Messiah. She stands as an engaged Bride, awaiting the future marriage to her Bridegroom. Four primary passages in the New Testament highlight this reality, all affirming that while the Church is espoused, her final union with Christ is still to come.

A. The Betrothal — (2 Corinthians 11:2)

Here, the Apostle Paul declares,

"For I am jealous over you with a godly jealousy: for I

espoused you to one husband, that I might present you as a pure virgin to Christ."

Addressing the local congregation in Corinth, Paul emphasizes that through evangelism, they have been betrothed (i.e., espoused) to one Husband, ultimately to be presented as a pure virgin to the Messiah. This will be brought about through the process of sanctification.

Unlike Israel, who was found guilty of spiritual adultery, the coming union between the Church and her Messiah will reveal a Bride who is wholly pure.

68. "Espoused you to one husband" (11:2). How is "the simplicity that is in Christ" (11:3) related to this?

____

____

B. The Process of Preparation (Sanctification and Maturing) — (Ephesians 5:25-27)

"Husbands, love your wives, even as Christ also loved the church, and gave himself for it; That he might sanctify and cleanse it with the washing of water by the word, That he might present it to himself a glorious church, not having spot, or wrinkle, or any such thing; but that it should be holy and without blemish."

The Messiah's deep love for the Church is demonstrated through His sacrificial death on her behalf. One key purpose behind His atoning work is to sanctify the Church, ensuring that she may be presented as a pure virgin, as portrayed in 1 Corinthians 11:2. This sanctification comes about through continual cleansing by the water of the Word, underscoring the necessity of Scripture in shaping and purifying believers. Here, the *"water"* is not the water of baptism; it is the Word of God, which carries out a spiritual, cleansing ministry.

Through this ongoing process of sanctification, the Church is progressively prepared to stand without spot or wrinkle, holy and blameless before the Messiah. When the work is complete, He will receive unto Himself a radiant Bride—utterly free from any trace of defilement, corruption, or sin.

69. As you look at 5:25–32, what can you find in this section about how Christ

loved the church?

____

____

70. We sometimes forget that Christ is head of the church as we get bogged down in local church business, politics, or ministry. Since we are all in the role of "*bride*" when it comes to our relationship to Christ, what are some ways your local church can be more submissive to Christ?

____

____

C. The Celebration of the Marriage Supper of the Lamb — (Rev. 19:6–9)

In order to grasp the full meaning of Revelation 19:6–9, we must first understand the four stages of the traditional Jewish wedding system—common in our Lord's day and used among many Jewish communities even into the last century. All four phases, as rightly observed by Dr. Arnold Fruchtenbaum, are found in the Church's relationship as the Bride of the Messiah.

Stage One: The Arrangement

In the Jewish custom, the father of the groom would arrange the marriage and pay the bride price. This could occur at any point—sometimes long before the actual wedding day, or even just a short while prior to the ceremony. Because so much time could pass between the first and second stages, the bride and groom often would not see one another until the wedding itself.

Likewise, in the Church's relationship to the Messiah, our heavenly Father arranged for the Bride and provided the bride price—namely, the blood of Christ, as described in Ephesians 5:25–27. While the price has already been paid, the remaining three stages are yet future.

Stage Two: Fetching the Bride

After a substantial interval, the groom would go to the bride's home and bring her to his own. Often accompanied by a procession, this event was known as "fetching the bride." In parallel, though nearly two thousand years have elapsed since the Church's bride price was paid, the second stage will yet occur: the Messiah will come to take His Bride home.

We refer to this as the Rapture of the Church (1 Thessalonians 4:13–18). The Church will be *"caught up"* to *"meet the Lord in the air,"* thus completing the second stage prior to the Tribulation.

Stage Three: The Marriage Ceremony

Once the Bride was brought to the groom's house, a marriage ceremony would follow, attended by only a select few. Revelation 19:6–8 indicates that for the Church, this ceremony will take place in Heaven just before the Messiah's Second Coming at the conclusion of the Tribulation. At that time, the wedding announcement will be proclaimed, and the Bride—made ready through sanctification—will be clothed in *"fine linen, bright and pure,"* representing the righteous acts of the saints. This assures us that every unworthy work (wood, hay, stubble) will have been removed at the Judgment Seat of Christ (1 Corinthians 3:10–15), leaving only what is precious in God's sight.

Stage Four: The Marriage Feast

Finally, following the ceremony, the wedding feast would often last up to seven days. Revelation 19:9 refers to this *"marriage supper of the Lamb,"* distinguishing it from the ceremony by noting the many guests invited. We know Old Testament saints and Tribulation saints are resurrected at the close of the Tribulation (Daniel 12:2), and John the Baptist, who called himself the friend of the Bridegroom (John 3:27–30), falls under the category of these Old Testament saints. Thus, these resurrected believers will be the *"many"* who are invited to the marriage feast on earth.

While the wedding ceremony transpires in Heaven, the marriage feast will occur on earth after the Messiah's Second Coming and likely inaugurates the Millennial Kingdom. In this way, all four stages of the Jewish wedding system will be fulfilled in the union of the Church and her Bridegroom—beginning with the arrangement and purchase, culminating in the joyful feast that opens the Messianic Age.

So then, we can see how this passage (Rev. 19:6-9) shows us the Bride already in Heaven, and how that this scene transpires after the Church has been raptured. The fine, white linen she wears is described to John as representing the righteous acts of the saints. This scene follows the Judgment Seat of Christ, where every work of *"wood, hay, and stubble"* is consumed. Everything of *"gold, silver, and precious stone"* is refined, leaving only those righteous deeds to adorn the Bride (cf. Rom. 14:10–12; 1 Cor. 3:10–15; 2 Cor. 5:10). Having been raptured and sanctified, she now enters into the marriage ceremony, thereby becoming the Wife of the Messiah.

71. Why did the great multitude urge everyone to be happy? How? (19:6–7)

72. *"His wife"* (19:7). Who is the Lamb's bride (Ephesians 5:23–32)?

73. In what ways did the bride get ready for the heavenly wedding? (19:7–8)

74. What is the significance of the fine linen worn by the bride of Christ? (19:8)

75. Who is called *"blessed"*? (19:9)

76. How would you describe the mood in heaven when judgment is done and God prepares to unite believers with Him forever?

77. What does *"hallelujah"* mean?

78. Why do you think *"hallelujah"* is repeated again and again in heaven?

79. What is the value in praising God?

80. What are some of the ways we can praise God?

81. What is one psalm, hymn, or spiritual song that summarizes how you feel about God?

82. What difference does it make to you that God's judgments are true and just?

83. What are some implications of the fact that Christ's relationship with the church is described as a marriage?

84. In what ways ought we to act as people *"espoused"* (e.g., engaged) to Christ?

85. How intimate should your life in Christ be, in view of the metaphor of bride and groom?

---

86. How should this relationship affect your daily walk?

---

87. To what extent are our *"wedding garments"* earned, and to what extent are they a gift?

---

88. Who does God invite to the wedding supper of the Lamb? How?

---

89. What is one way you could become a more worshipful person in how you participate in worship services at church?

D. The Bride's Everlasting Joy of Dwelling in the New Jerusalem — (Rev. 21:9–22:5)

Revelation 21:9–22:5 reveals the Bride's final, everlasting dwelling place. Verses 9b–10 record:

> *"And he spake with me, saying, Come hither, I will shew thee the bride, the Lamb's wife. And he carried me away in the Spirit to a great and high mountain, and shewed me that great city, the holy Jerusalem, descending out of heaven from God."*

The closing chapters of the Bible provide the final portrait of the Messiah's Bride. Here, in light of the four preceding stages of the Jewish wedding system, we see that the Bride is now referred to as the Lamb's Wife. In Revelation 21:10–22:5, Scripture offers a vivid description of her eternal splendor and the glorious dwelling place she will share with the Lamb forever. When John was caught up, he beheld the eternal New Jerusalem and describes this holy city in detail, reassuring John and his readership that the Bride and Wife of the Messiah will reside there throughout all eternity. Although there will be a temporary earthly home during the Messianic Kingdom, her ultimate and permanent habitation will be in the New Jerusalem.

90. *"Lamb"* (21:9). "Lamb" is a key word in Revelation. Why?

____

____

91. *"Great and high mountain"* (21:10). Compare this with the place from which John had viewed Babylon in the earlier vision of 17:3 ff.

____

____

92. What were some of the more spectacular features of the New Jerusalem that John saw? (21:10–21)

____

____

93. In what way will the New Jerusalem reflect God's glory and holiness? (21:21–27)

____

____

94. What did John discover about the temple in the New Jerusalem? (21:22)

____

____

95. What will be the New Jerusalem's source of light? (21:23–24)

____

____

96. How did John describe the New Jerusalem in terms of safety or security?

(21:25)

____

____

97. How did John describe the heavenly city in terms of purity? (21:26–27)

____

____

98. Whose names are on each of these:
TWELVE GATES:

____

____

99. TWELVE FOUNDATIONS:

____

____

100. What do you observe from these additional related passages: Hebrews 11:10, 16; 12:22–24, 28; Revelation 7:9, 13–17; 1 Peter 1:4; 2 Peter 3:13; Revelation 4:1–3; Revelation 22:14?

____

____

Conclusion

This study concludes our exploration of what the Scriptures reveal concerning the Wife of Jehovah and the Bride of the Messiah—thus also concluding our series on *The Four Women of the Apocalypse*. We began with Jezebel, the Spiritual Adulteress of Thyatira; then beheld the glory of the Woman clothed with the sun in Revelation 12, representing the mother of the Messiah in Israel; next, we examined the doom of the Great Harlot, Babylon, whose fate is sealed due to her spiritual and ecumenical fornication; and finally, we turned to the most beautiful of all, the Bride of the Messiah—His blood-bought Church, espoused and awaiting the heavenly wedding ceremony when she shall be forever united to the Lamb of God, which taketh away the sin of the world.

Among the various ways that Scripture keeps Israel and the Church distinct, this study offers one of the most vivid. Attempting to conflate Israel, the Wife of Jehovah, with the Church, the Bride of the Messiah, leads inevitably to confusion and contradictions due to the unique descriptions each receives. It is only when we recognize them as separate entities—Israel as Jehovah's Wife and the Church as Messiah's Bride—that these apparent contradictions are resolved.

~ THE END ~

CHAPTER FIVE

Appendix A

Purity Is Power

Revelation 2:18–29

Introduction:

Main Thought: Protect yourself from becoming corrupted by carnality and pursue purity constrained by Christ's compassion.

I. A Pastor Commended by Christ (Rev. 2:18-19).

A. Attributes of Christ & His Local Church (Rev. 2:18).

1. The Servants of God in Thyatira (v. 18a)

2. The Son of God (v. 18b).

a. His Piercing Eyes

b. His Punishing Feet

B. Acknowledgments by Christ (Rev. 2:19).

1. A Working, Loving, Serving, Believing, Enduring, Hard Working Pastor (v. 19a).

2. A Pastor Who Wants His Last Works to Be His Best Works (v. 19b).

II. A Pastor Corrupted By Carnality (Rev. 2:20-23).

A. The Lord Says, "Because..." (Rev. 2:20-21).

1. The Lustful Suffering of Jezebel (v. 20).

a. The Dangers of Role-Reversal - Teaching God's Servants to Sin

b. The Dangers of a Self-proclaimed Prophet - Leading God's Servants into Idolatry

2. The Longsuffering of Jesus (v. 21).

a. The Lord Gives "Space to Repent"

b. Lustful Rebellion Refuses to Repent

B. The Lord Says, "Behold..." (Rev. 2:22-23).

1. The Casting of Sin's Consequences (v. 22).

a. Gross Disease - The Bed of Sin Becomes the Bed of Sickness (v. 22a).

b. Great Distress - The Adulterers Afflictions - Lamentable Distress (v. 22b).

c. Grievous Death - The Wages of Sin Is Death (v. 22c).

2. What the Churches Shall Know (v. 23).

a. Their Omniscience Judge (v. 23a).

b. His Objective Justice (v. 23b).

III. A Purity Constrained By Compassion (Rev. 2:24-25).

A. The Faithful Remnant (Rev. 2:24).

1. Where They Are: (v. 24a)

a. Among the Lord's Local Churches in General

b. Within the Lord's Local Church in Particular

2. How They Are Discerned: (v. 24b)

a. Not Deviating in THIS Doctrine (see above)

b. Not Delving the Depths of the Devil

B. Encouraged to Remain Faithful (Rev. 2:25).

1. True to the Sacred Scriptures (v. 25a).

2. True till His Second Coming (v. 25b).

IV. A Power Crowning the Conqueror (Rev. 2:26-29).

A. The Condition - (Rev. 2:26a).

1. Keep on Overcoming

2. Keep on Keeping Christ's Works Till the End

B. The Crown (Rev. 2:26b-27).

1. Its Significance - POWER (v. 26b).

2. Its Shepherding - ROD (v. 27a).

3. Its Source - The FATHER (v. 27b).

C. Christ Himself - The Morning Star (Rev. 2:28).

Conclusion:

"He that hath an ear, let him hear what the Spirit saith unto the churches."

CHAPTER SIX

Appendix B

Two Wonders

Revelation 12:1–6

Introduction:

> *And there appeared a great wonder in heaven; a woman clothed with the sun, and the moon under her feet, and upon her head a crown of twelve stars: And she being with child cried, travailing in birth, and pained to be delivered. And there appeared another wonder in heaven; and behold a great red dragon, having seven heads and ten horns, and seven crowns upon his heads. And his tail drew the third part of the stars of heaven, and did cast them to the earth: and the dragon stood before the woman which was ready to be delivered, for to devour her child as soon as it was born. And she brought forth a man child, who was to rule all nations with a rod of iron: and her child was caught up unto God, and to his throne. And the woman fled into the wilderness, where she hath a place prepared of God, that they should feed her there a thousand two hundred and threescore days.*
>
> Revelation 12:1–6

Oliver B. Greene highlights the prominence of the number seven throughout the book of Revelation, symbolizing God's divine completeness. He points out several groups of sevens: the seven churches in chapters 2 and 3, the seven-sealed book in chapter 5, the seven seals beginning in chapter 6, the seven trumpets starting in chapter 8, the seven personages in chapters 12 and 13, the seven vials in chapter 16, the seven dooms in chapters 17 through 19, and the seven new things in chapters 21 and 22.

According to Greene, Revelation illustrates the completion of God's plan, making an end to sin and sorrow and fulfilling His work of redemption for all creation. Just as Paradise was lost in the early chapters of Genesis, it is restored with even greater glory in the final chapters of Revelation (21 and 22).

Main Thought: Has God forgotten Israel? Absolutely not!

As was observed by Dr. Adrian Rogers, let me tell you, these are perilous times we're living in. The storm clouds are gathering, the lightning is flashing, and the lightning rod is Israel. Today, Israel is featured in headlines across major news outlets and platforms worldwide. As Bible-believing Christians, we cannot ignore the significance of this tiny nation. If you open your Bible and carefully read the prophecies, you'll see that Israel is at the center of every prophecy about the future.

The eyes of the world are on Israel, and our eyes need to be there as well, because Israel and the Jewish people are the people and land of destiny. As goes Israel, so goes the world. Israel is God's yardstick, His measuring rod, His blueprint, and His program for what He is doing on the world stage.

So we have to ask: ***Has God turned His back on Israel? Has He forgotten them?*** Has He canceled the promises He made to Abraham, Isaac, and Jacob? Absolutely not! The passage we're looking at today speaks directly to the nation of Israel, and from Revelation 12, we're going to consider some important truths about Israel this morning.

Chapter 12 begins with these striking words in verses 1 and 2: *"And there appeared a great wonder in heaven; a woman clothed with the sun, and the moon under her feet, and upon her head a crown of twelve stars: And she being with child cried, travailing in birth, and pained to be delivered."* This woman, described as a *"great wonder,"* is clothed in a truly remarkable way. She is adorned with the sun, with the moon beneath her feet, and wearing a crown of twelve stars as her headdress. She is also an expectant mother, and her time to give birth is near.

I. The Radiant Woman (Rev. 12:1-2).

- **Woman = Israel**
- **Woman Does not equal Mary (Rev. 12:13-17 — persecuted during Tribulation)**
- **Second of four "women" in the Revelation**
    - Rev. 2:20- Jezebel
    - Rev. 12:1- Israel
    - Rev. 17:4- the Harlot
    - Rev. 19:7- Bride, Lambs wife
- **Satan hates Israel**

A. Her Clothing (Rev. 12:1a).

1. The Sun About Her

2. The Moon Beneath Her

B. Her Crown (Rev. 12:1b).

- Twelve Starry Jewels (Genesis 37:9–11)

C. Her Cries (Rev. 12:2).

1. The Baby in Her Womb (v. 2a).

2. Her Birth-pangs of Labor (v. 2b) (cf., Isaiah 9:6; Micah 5:2–3; Romans 9:4–5; John 4:22; Isaiah 66:7–9).

> But praise God, Jesus fulfilled every demand of God the Father, He paid sin's debt in its fulness. He conquered death, hell and the grave. He arose, He appeared to men, He ascended back to the Father and He is coming again in power and great glory. Jesus will personally supervise putting Satan into the lake of fire, where he will be tormented with fire and brimstone forever and ever.[1]

II. The Red Dragon (Rev. 12:3-4).

- **Red = Bloodthirsty**

A. His Infamous Power (Rev. 12:3).

1. Seven Crowned Heads

2. Ten Horns (Rev. 13:1)

---

[1] Oliver B. Greene, *Revelation, A Verse by Verse Study*, The Gospel Hour, Inc., 1963, 240–241.

- Power behind Antichrist

- Crowns (i.e., *diadems*)- authority / Power (limited)

B. His Influencing Pride (Rev. 12:4a).

1. Drawn

2. Downcast

   - Tail swept 1/3 “stars” threw- aorist, completed action

     - Meteors? (perhaps)

     - 1/3 of the angels

     - Nations? Probably not. (Job 38:7; Ezekiel 28:15; 2 Peter 2:4; Jude 6)

C. His Insatiable Passion (Rev. 12:4b).

1. Behold, Satan Is At the Door

2. He Seeks to Devour (1 Pet. 5:8)

III. The Raptured Prince (Rev. 12:5-6).

A. The Rightful Heir (Rev. 12:5a; Matt. 2:13).

- The Shepherd's Iron Rod (see Ps. 2; 22-24; specifically, Ps. 2:9; Rev. 2:27; 19:15; Gal. 4:4-5)

B. His Rapture to God (Rev. 12:5b).

- The Ascension of the Son of God to Glory (see Acts 1; specifically, Acts 1:10-11; Eph. 1:20-23)

C. His Runaway Mother (Rev. 12:6).

1. Her Place of Refuge - the Desert/Wilderness

2. God's Preparation for Her

3. The Time of Her Provision - 1260 days

   - Fails to destroy Christ, turns devious attention to woman (persecuted especially in the last 3 ½ years)

     - Details of Tribulation persecution (Rev. 12:13-17)

I was talking to some Jewish friends, and they said, "You Christians ought not to try to proselytize Jews." I said, "Friend, you proselytized me. I serve a Jewish Messiah." Israel gave Jesus to this world, and I thank God for it. What I'm talking about is Israel's special favor. Listen to me. Israel is a God-ordained, God-called, God-protected, and God-blessed nation. Why did God call and ordain Israel—to make them a blessing alone? No. That through Israel all the world would be blessed. Put this scripture down—Genesis chapter 12 and verse 3. God is speaking to Abraham. God is saying, "Abraham, I'm going to make a great nation of you," and here's what God said: *"And I will bless them that bless thee, and curse him that curseth thee: and in thee"*—Abraham—"shall all [the nations] of the [world] be blessed" (Genesis 12:3). I stand here today blessed because of Israel. I hold in my hand a Jewish book. I serve a Jewish Messiah, the Lord Jesus Christ. And God has made Abraham a blessing to all the nations of the world. And I want to tell you, my dear friend, you are very foolish and on shaky and dangerous ground if you pronounce a curse upon Israel. I'll tell you something else. When you bless what God has blessed, when you love what God has loved, then God is going to bless you. Now put this verse down—Deuteronomy chapter 7 and verse 6. We're talking about Israel's special favor. Here it is. Listen. God said to Israel, *"For thou art an holy people unto the LORD thy God: the LORD thy God hath chosen thee to be a special people unto himself, above all people that are upon the face of the earth"* (Deuteronomy 7:6). If you would be wise, you would learn to bless and not to curse Israel. Our evangelical, Bible-believing Christians need to pray for and love the nation Israel. Do you hear me? And our Jewish friends need to learn that the best friends they have on the face of this earth are Bible-believing Christians. And may the devil not muddy the water. We speak here of Israel's special favor.[2]

Conclusion:

---

[2] Adrian Rogers, "Why I Love Israel," *Adrian Rogers Sermon Archive*, 2017, Re 12.

Does this encourage you? It fills my heart with joy—yes, even makes me want to shout—to know that God has a plan. He has not abandoned His ancient people. God has blessed Israel so that they might be a blessing to the entire world. And one day, a fountain will be opened to them.

There is a fountain filled with blood

Drawn from Emmanuel's veins;

And sinners plunged beneath that flood

Lose all their guilty stains.

—William Cowper

How can we go through life, day after day, indifferent and complacent, in these significant and urgent times, without giving everything we have to Jesus Christ? How can we not love Him with a fervent, passionate, and wholehearted devotion? We are called to love what God loves. God loves His Son, Jesus—and so do I. God loves His chosen people—and so do I. He blessed Israel so that they might be a blessing to the entire world. And every time I see a son or daughter of Abraham, I find myself thinking, "Oh, if only they knew their Messiah, the Lord Jesus Christ."

But thank God, the day is coming—and it may not be far off—when all of this will unfold. I am so grateful for His Word. I'm grateful for the truth He reveals to us in Scripture. As I've said before, I may not have every detail perfectly understood, because some things are difficult to see and interpret. But this I know without a doubt: Jesus is Lord, and He's coming again. Praise His name!

CHAPTER SEVEN

Appendix C

The Terrible War

Revelation 12:7–12

INTRODUCTION

ILLUSTRATION

The Bible is a book of blood … wholly distinct from all other books for just one reason, namely, that it contains blood circulating through every page and in every verse. From Genesis to Revelation we see the stream of blood. Everything about the death of Christ was bloody—the slapping of his face must have cut his face; the scourge ripped apart his back; the crown of thorns pierced his brow; blood from his hands and ankles spurted with every blow of the hammer; blood likely oozed from his nose and mouth as he writhed on the cross; blood and water gushed from his side when the lance tore him open. It was not a bloodless death. It was a death designed to paint the cross crimson.[3]

MAIN THOUGHT

STRIVE TO WIN SOULS FROM SATAN'S SINKING SHIP; CONQUER THE DEVIL THROUGH FAITH IN CHRIST!

Connecting Context: Review the context of Chapter 12 - Three Wonders: The Radiant Woman; The Red Dragon; The Raptured Prince.

- I am very tired, but must go on ... A fire is in my bones ... Oh God, what can I say? Souls! Souls! Souls! My heart hungers for souls! ~ General William Booth
- I would rather win souls than be the greatest king or emperor on earth; I would rather win souls than be the greatest general that ever commanded an army; I would rather win souls than be the greatest poet, or novelist, or literary man who ever walked the earth. My one ambition in life is to win as many as possible. ~ R. A. Torrey
- There is a power which lies at the center of all success in preaching, and whose influence reaches out to the circumference, and is essential everywhere. Without its presence we cannot imagine the most brilliant talents making a preacher of the Gospel in the fullest sense. Where it is largely present, it is wonderful how many deficiencies count for nothing ... The power is the value of the human soul, felt by the preacher and inspiring all his work. ~ Phillips Brooks, in Lectures on Preaching[4]

I. The War in Heaven (Rev. 12:7-9).

A. The Opponents (Rev. 12:7-8).

---

[3] M. R. DeHaan, *The Chemistry of the Blood* (Grand Rapids: Zondervan, 1943), 13, quoted in Robert J. Morgan, *Nelson's Complete Book of Stories, Illustrations, and Quotes*, electronic ed. (Nashville: Thomas Nelson, 2000), 76–77.

[4] Robert J. Morgan, 85.

1. The Captains (Rev. 12:7).

a. Of the Armies of Heaven (v. 7a).

"Michael and his angels fought." Who is Michael? He is leading the army of angels who are battling Satan and his angels. Michael is mentioned five times in the Scriptures: (Daniel 10:13-21; Daniel 12:1; Jude 9; Revelation 12:7). He seems to be the highest of all angels. Jude calls him THE archangel. Read I Thessalonians 4:16 and Jude 9. It seems that Michael is the leading angel having to do with the Jewish people . . . he is probably the guardian angel over God's elect: *"And at that time shall Michael stand up, the great prince which standeth for the children of thy people"* (Daniel 12:1). That refers to Israel. Michael shall stand up to see that Israel does not perish in the Great Tribulation - the time of Jacob's trouble. *"He* (Jacob) *shall be saved out of it"* (Jeremiah 30:7). Michael is the militant angel who fights on the side of God's elect-Israel. . . . The struggle between light and darkness, though invisible, is nevertheless real. Read I Samuel 16:13-15, I Kings 22:19-23. Angels and angelic influence toward Christians here on earth is accepted by most spiritual people as a Bible fact. I believe that every born again person has a guardian angel (Acts 12, Hebrews 1:14). Angels watch over little children (Matthew 18:10).[5]

b. Of the Enemies from Hell (v. 7b).

The biblical teaching that an attack against the Lord's creation, including His angels and His people, is an attack against Christ is foundational to the understanding of this battle. For instance, when the Lord Jesus Christ stopped Saul of Tarsus on the

---

[5] Oliver B. Greene, *Revelation, A Verse by Verse Study,* (The Gospel Hour, Inc., 1963), 252–253.

Damascus road, He asked the poignant question, *"Saul, Saul, why persecutest thou me? I am Jesus whom thou persecutest..."* (Acts 9:4-5). Saul had previously led in the stoning of Stephen and attacked the Jerusalem church (Acts 7-8), and the Saviour revealed that it was really an attack upon Him. Since Jehovah had put *"enmity"* between the seed of the serpent (the Antichrist) and the seed of the woman (Christ), Satan has attacked both Christ directly and His creation indirectly through the centuries (cf. Gen. 3:15). The great red dragon had failed in his efforts against the precious Lord Jesus, and now his attack was upon the Jewish remnant. In order to overcome the woman, the dragon needed to defeat the woman's protecting angel—Michael, as Daniel predicted, saying, *"And at that time shall Michael stand up, the great prince which standeth for the children of thy people: and there shall be a time of trouble, such as never was since there was a nation even to that same time: and at that time thy people shall be delivered, every one that shall be found written in the book"* (cf. Dan. 12:1).[6]

2. The Combat (Rev. 12:8).

a. The Dragon Overpowered (v. 8a; cf. Job 25:1-2).

b. The Dragon Ousted (v. 8b).

Apparently, Satan and his demons had a place around the thrown of God, as Micaiah stated, saying, *"And he said, Hear thou therefore the word of the LORD: I saw the LORD sitting on his throne, and all the host of heaven standing by him on his right hand and on his left"* (I Ki. 22:19). John used the second aorist passive form of eurisko to denote that the Lord did not find their

---

[6] Thomas M. Strouse, *To the Seven Churches: A Commentary on the Apocalypse of Jesus Christ*, (Bible Baptist Theological Press, 2013), 483.

place and therefore excluded the satanic host from His presence. He intensified the expulsion with the little adverb éti ("any more") to show that the heavenly exclusion was thorough and final. For the first time since Lucifer's fall, heaven will have respite from the presence and antagonism of God's archenemy.[7]

The greater question however is when this battle takes place. Several views are generally advanced. The first is that the war in question took place when Satan rebelled against God in ages past resulting in their expulsion from heaven. Another view is that the war in question is conflict in heaven between Satan and God during the Tribulation. This view posits the position that Satan apparently has still been allowed access before God down through the ages as the accuser of the brethren. See Job 1. A third view is that there has been a spiritual war going on ever since Satan rebelled against God and continues to this day. The war will come to a head during the Tribulation when Satan is no longer allowed access to heaven. Though this is not the final climactic battle with Satan, it is significant in the scope of the Tribulation in that Satan's wrath is taken out against God's people on the earth. This third view is the likely position as the following text will show.[8]

B. The Outcome (Rev. 12:9).

- **Note** - This occurs at the Mid-point of the Tribulation

1. The Dragon's Description (v. 9a; cf. Isa. 27:1; 51:9; Ezek. 29:3).

---

[7] Thomas Strouse, 487.

[8] David H. Sorenson, *Understanding the Bible, An Independent Baptist Commentary* (Northstar Ministries, 2007), 458–459.

a. Archaic Serpent (cf., Gen. 3:1; Matt. 23:33; 2 Cor. 11:3).

Subtlety, craft and deep cunning are characteristic features of Satan from the beginning of his history in connection with the human race. I am satisfied that Genesis 3 is a true and actual account of what took place in the Garden of Eden. I believe Satan spoke through a real serpent. There is no need supposing that such is an impossibility, because it is not. There are at least three remarkable instances in the Old Testament where lower animals were given miraculous use of the power of speech. Speech was given to the serpent (Genesis 3). A certain intelligence and speech were granted to Balaam's ass (Numbers 22:21-30). The great fish which swallowed Jonah answered to the voice of the Lord God and disgorged the penitent prophet on dry ground (Jonah 2:10). I firmly believe in the exact historical accuracy of these narratives, which moreover are vouched for in the New Testament (II Corinthians 11:3; II Peter 2:15,16; Matthew 12:40).[9]

b. Diabolical Opposer (cf., 1 Chron. 21:1).

- **Note** - *Dia* + *Ballw* = to throw through, or to slander; see Job 1-2 for a Biblical Case Study on the Slander of Satan.

- **Note** - on Satan, also see Zech. 3:1-2:

c. Ecumenical Deceiver (cf., John 8:44).

- **Note** - Dr. Thomas Strouse points out the danger

---

[9] Oliver B. Greene, 255.

of ecumenism well:

οἰκουμένην – This is the Greek source for the Latin oecumenicus and English "ecumenical" meaning "inhabited house." The ecumenical movement is a diabolical effort to unite all "divisions" of Christendom into one universal conglomerate of theological heresies, and described by the Revelator as "Babylon the great, the mother of harlots" (Rev. 17:5).[10]

2. The Dragon Downcast (v. 9b).

a. The Great Dragon Cast Down.

b. Cast Down into the Earth.

c. His Angels Cast Down With Him.

Application: Judgments of Satan:

HAS SATAN BEEN JUDGED OR WILL HE BE?

Satan has been judged and he will be judged again. There are at least six judgments which Satan has experienced or will experience: (1) He was barred from his original privileged position in heaven (Eze 28:16). (2) A judgment was pronounced on him in the Garden of Eden after the temptation of Adam and Eve (Gen 3:14–15). (3) The central judgment (because it is the basis of all others) was at the cross (Jn 12:31). (4) He will be barred from all access to heaven during the tribulation period (Rev 12:13). (5) At the beginning of the millennium he will be confined in the abyss (not, as incorrectly translated, bottomless pit) (Rev 20:2). (6) At the conclusion of the millennium he will be cast into the lake of fire for all

[10] Thomas Strouse, Footnote #1894.

eternity (Rev 20:10).[11]

Now when I was studying and preparing this message, I thought to myself, "You know, Satan's on his way down." First of all, he is cast out of his lofty mountain where he was the anointed cherub, ministering praise to God, but still given access. And now that limited access is taken from Satan, and he's cast down to the earth. But soon he's going to be cast into the bottomless pit, the abyss. And soon he's going to be taken out of the abyss and put into the lowest hell, and that's where he will spend eternity, in the lowest hell, and he won't be ruling there in hell. The one who said, "I will exalt myself above the stars of God" (Isaiah 14:13) will be brought down into the lowest hell. And if you're following him, you'll be there with him. Hell was prepared for the devil and his angels (Matthew 25:41). Why follow a loser? Friend, I'm following the Lord Jesus Christ.[12]

Transition: I regret to inform you that there's a Terrible War that's going on in Heaven, but now, I've got the latest update for you about how the conflict of the ages is going, and I'm thrilled to bring you-

II. The Word from Heaven (Rev. 12:10-12).

A. God's Kingdom Is Come (Rev. 12:10).

1. The Awe (v. 10a).

a. Salvation.

---

[11] Charles Caldwell Ryrie, *A Survey of Bible Doctrine* (Chicago: Moody Press, 1972).

[12] Adrian Rogers, "Why I Love Israel," in *Adrian Rogers Sermon Archive* (Signal Hill, CA: Rogers Family Trust, 2017), Re 12.

b. Power (Capability).

c. Kingdom.

d. Authority (cf., 1 Cor. 15:27-28).

2. The Accuser (v. 10b).

a. His Betrayal Squashed (cf., Rom. 8:28-39).

b. His Accusations Endless (cf., 1 John 2:1-2).

B. God's Will Is Done in Heaven (Rev. 12:11-12a).

1. Faith Is the Victory (Rev. 12:11a).

- **Note -** 3 Keys to Victory: (they = believers)
    - **Basis -** The Blood of the Lamb (the Work of Christ)
    - **Activity -** Testimony/Witness
    - **Attitude -** Complete Self-sacrifice - Willing to die

"Seeming defeat is ultimate victory." ~ Dr. Charles Ryrie, p. 92

a. The Believer's Conquest - The Blood of the Lamb

(cf., Gen. 3:20-21; 4:4; Isa. 53:5-7; Heb. 11:28).

- **Note** - the Doctrine of the Blood of Christ the Lamb of God throughout Revelation: Rev. 1:5; 5:9; 7:14; see also 1 Jn. 5:5.

b. The Believer's Confession - The Word of Their Testimony (cf., 2 Thess. 2:13; Jn. 18:37).

2. The Believer's Courage - Devoted to the Death (Rev. 12:11b; cf., Jn. 12:25; Matt. 10:28-30).

These brethren in that day overcome (get the victory) over the devil by (a) *"the blood of the Lamb"* and (b) *"the word of their testimony."* Powerful is the effect of the blood of the Lamb in the battle against Satan. Even in this day, it is a powerful deterrent to Satan's influence. It absolutely protects us in our position in Christ. Pleading the blood also brings victory over temptation and other Satanic influence. Moreover, the word of our testimony is a powerful deterrent to Satanic influence. Clearly implied is outspoken testifying. It is taking the offensive spiritually. It gives direct victory over Satan's power. Moreover, the brethren in that day will love not their lives unto the death. They will be willing to have their heads removed for the name of Jesus.[13]

3. The Believer's Choir - Rejoicing in the Heavens (Rev. 12:12a).

- **Note** - plural to show that Satan is NOWHERE to be found in all the heavens which includes: 2 Cor. 12:4; Lk. 23:43; Rev. 2:7; Jn. 14:3; 2 Cor. 5:8;

---

[13] David H. Sorenson, 460.

Phil. 1:21; Rev. 11:15.

C. Satan's Wrath Is Upon the Earth (Rev. 12:12b).

1. Description of Woe (cf., Rev. 8:13).

2. Diabolical Wrath.

The reason for this first woe is that *"the devil"* ...*"is come down"* ... to the earth inhabitants. This descent corresponds to Satan's fall from heaven as a star when the Fifth Trumpet Judgment (= First Woe Judgment) sounded (cf. Rev. 9:1ff.).[14]

- **Note -** Present active participle from the root *ekw* speaks of perpetual possession

3. Disappearing Window of Time.

CONCLUSION

Summary/Review: The Terrible War - The Bad Guys Don't Always Win - The Lord's Army Is Greater than the Devil's - The Devil Is a Sore Loser - One day, he's going to take his wrath out on the earth, middle way through the Tribulation - He's doomed to the Abyss, and then the Lake of Fire - He only has a little time, and he knows it - Don't become one of his casualties - Don't let your loved ones be part of his casualty - There are souls to rescue from sin - How many are the souls that you will win? I'm On the Winning Side!

I'm grieved to tell you that there is a Terrible War in heaven, but I'm glad to report that the Tremendous Word from heaven is that WE WIN!

---

[14] Thomas Strouse, 497.

CHAPTER EIGHT

Appendix D

What Made the Devil So Mad

Revelation 12:13–17

Introduction:

Illustration -

Everlasting Arms, Overshadowing Wings

The best way to handle danger is simply to be where God tells you to be. When physician L. Nelson Bell and his wife Virginia felt God calling them to China as missionaries, they gave scant thought to danger. It came upon them nonetheless in the form of the Japanese invasion of China. The Bells were in Tsingkiangpu, the provincial capital of Kiangsu, and the enemy advanced against them from all four directions. Older missionaries urged the Bells to flee, for the Japanese were known for their cruelty.

But Dr. Bell had been studying the Old Testament, especially Psalms, Proverbs, and Isaiah, and he developed a strong conviction that it was God's will for them to remain in Tsingkiangpu. Virginia agreed, writing to her mother in America, "The children are just as happy as can be, and if things come to worst here, I'm going to stick right with them and keep them happily engaged. Our God is able, and that 'Restraining Hand' is all-loving and all-powerful."

Dr. Bell later wrote that the decision to remain "deepened and confirmed our sense of the closeness of God. He was right there with us. Underneath with everlasting arms, over us with overshadowing wings —we were conscious of His peace and presence in a way that I don't think we would ever have been otherwise. There was prayer, constant prayer, in our heart. And also constant thanksgiving and praise for the consciousness of His presence. You had no one else to depend on. It was a sense of safety within His keeping."[15]

Main Thought:
The servants of God will be secured by God accomplish His purposes upon the earth.

Sub-intro: Explain the Context - The war in heaven has led to the expulsion of the dragon who now brings his war upon the earth.

I. The Dragon's Focused Fierceness (Rev. 12:13).

A. His Perception of Judgment (v. 13a).

Having been defeated by the perfect life of the Saviour, His work on the cross, subsequent death, resurrection and ascension, and now by expulsion from Heaven, the Devil focused his wrath on the nation through whom his Victor came.[16]

---

[15] Robert J. Morgan, *Nelson's Complete Book of Stories, Illustrations, and Quotes,* electronic ed. (Nashville: Thomas Nelson Publishers, 2000), 381–382.

[16] Thomas M. Strouse, *To the Seven Churches: A Commentary on the Apocalypse of Jesus Christ,* (Bible Baptist Theological Press, 2013), 499.

B. His Persecution of the Woman (v. 13b).

- **Note -** this persecution of the Jewish nation is all according to the Lord's prediction: Matt. 24:21; 15-20; Lk. 21:20-21.

II. The Woman's Flight to Freedom (Rev. 12:14).

A. On Eagles' Wings (v. 14a; cf., Isa. 40:31; Exo. 19:4; Deut. 32:11).

B. Her Place of Nourishment (v. 14b).

- **Note** - the play on the word *"place"* within the text - candlestick's (Rev. 2:5), islands (Rev. 6:14), Woman (Rev. 12:6, 14), Angels (Rev. 12:8), Armageddon's (Rev. 16:16), & the Sinner's lack of a place (Rev. 20:11).

- **Note -** it is also passive "she is nourished"

- **Note -** Hebraic parallels between Rev. 12:6 and Rev. 12:14.

- **Note -** 3&1/2 years corresponds to - Dan. 7:25; 9:27; 12:7.

- **Note -** *"from the face of the serpent"* which offered

Eve such false hope now glares upon Israel with hateful wrath (cf., 2 Cor. 11:14).

III. The Dragon's Foul Flood (Rev. 12:15-16).

A. Intent on Drowning the Woman (Rev. 12:15).

- **Note -** Perhaps a fulfillment of - (though water may also be literal here, see Rev. 13:4, 11-14) Isa. 59:19; Lk. 21:20-24.

B. Intercepted by the Earth (Rev. 12:16).

- **Note -** word study on "helped" - see Matt. 15:25; Mk. 9:22, 24; Acts 16:9; 21:28; 2 Cor. 6:2; Heb. 2:18.

IV. The Dragon's Furious Fighting (Rev. 12:17).

A. Wrath Upon the Woman (v. 17a).

B. War with Her Remnant (v. 17b).

- **The Reasons -** Commandment Keepers & Witness Bearers

The divine protection given the woman enraged the dragon even more, but all he could do was redirect his animosity: ...The dragon had to redirect his anger from the Son to the woman in 12:5 when the Son escaped his clutches. That increased his rage. He lost his place in heaven in 12:8, 9, 12, angering him even more. At this point the woman has escaped to a place of refuge, leaving him only the woman's remaining seed to vent his fury on. The repeated frustration of his efforts explains the furious persecution the dragon proceeds to inflict on the faithful. He goes away "to make war with" ..."the rest of her seed" ...who apparently did not go with their fellow Israelites to the place of refuge. Besides the Son, the woman, earlier identified as national Israel, has other children who are distinguished from the group of Jewish people whom the dragon cannot touch. These are scattered followers of the Lamb who did not reach the appointed place in the wilderness prepared for the main body of people symbolized by the woman.[17]

This remnant are those who (1) "keep the commandments of God," and (2) "have the testimony of Jesus." These clearly are Jews converted to Christ. One of the great purposes of the Tribulation is precisely to that end. As the two witnesses preached and the 144,000 are converted, they in turn fan out preaching the gospel to the Jew first and then to any gentiles who will listen. It is clear that the Olivet Discourse as recorded in Matthew 24-25 and Luke 21 is directed to believing Jews in that day. They will have turned to Christ and are just beginning to explore the New Testament. The Holy Spirit, perhaps working through the 144,000 witnesses, may direct their attention to the Olivet Discourse to give them guidance as to what is taking place about them. It is to this remnant of believing Jews that the devil turns

[17] Robert L. Thomas, *Revelation 8-22: An Exegetical Commentary* (Chicago: Moody Publishers, 1995), 141.

the fury of His wrath.[18]

Conclusion:

The LORD will bring a remnant out of the Tribulation (cf. Isa. 10:20-22). Paul confirmed this truth, stating, *"Esaias also crieth concerning Israel, Though the number of the children of Israel be as the sand of the sea, a remnant shall be saved"* (Rom. 9:27). This saved remnant will enter into the Millennium as a nation born in a day, Isaiah predicted, saying, *"Before she travailed, she brought forth; before her pain came, she was delivered of a man child. Who hath heard such a thing? who hath seen such things? Shall the earth be made to bring forth in one day? or shall a nation be born at once? for as soon as Zion travailed, she brought forth her children"* (Isa. 66:7-8).[19]

- **Note** - The Chronology of the events of the prophecy of this chapter - 1. Messiah's Birth; 2. Tribulation; 3. Nation of Israel Born in a Day, at the outset of the Millennium

Therefore, when Israel became a nation on May 14th, 1948, it was NOT a fulfillment of this prophecy! What happens after the Dragon suffers ultimate failure here in Chapter 12? He will be imprisoned in the bottomless pit for a thousand years and then ultimately thrown into the Lake of Fire (Rev. 20:1-3, 10). As Croft Pentz noted, Satan is powerful, but God's power is greater. God is on our side no matter who is against us (Rom. 8:31). If God lives within us, we are greater than he (Satan) who is in the world. With God's power, we can overcome all sin and be what God wants us to be.

---

[18] David H. Sorenson, *Understanding the Bible, An Independent Baptist Commentary* (Northstar Ministries, 2007), 464.

[19] Thomas Strouse, 507.

CHAPTER NINE

Appendix E

Mystery (Babylon) Solved

Revelation 17:1-18

Introduction:

> *"These shall make war with the Lamb, and the Lamb shall overcome them: for he is Lord of lords, and King of kings: and they that are with him are called, and chosen, and faithful."*
>
> Revelation 17:14

Since the beginning of the feeble ascendency of mankind after the fall, he has sought another way to find fulfillment apart from the True God of the Bible.

Main Thought:
Little children, keep yourselves from idols.

I. The Warning of Judgment (Rev. 17:1-3a)

A. The Woman Introduced (Rev. 17:1)

B. The World-Wide Influence She Wields (Rev.

17:2)

C. The Wilderness from Where John Watches (Rev. 17:3a)

The vision that the Apostle John received harked back to the beginning of the Tribulation, and gave the chronology of the rise and fall of Satan's religious-political-economic system during the Tribulation. This false system based on the Old Serpent's pantheistic Gnosticism proffered and accepted in the Garden (cf. notes on Rev. 13), will flourish during the first half of the Tribulation as an attempt to re-enact the world-wide religious rebellion with the tower of Babylon (cf. Gen. 11:1-9). Shortly after the Rapture, Satan will usher in his religious ecumenical movement as the peace-making rider on the white horse (cf. Rev. 6:1-2). By the time of the mid-point of the Tribulation, the kings following the Antichrist will dump ecumenical Babylonianism and will worship the Beast directly and promote his economic Babylonianism (Rev. 17:16-18:24). Isaiah predicted the fall of Babylon centuries before, saying, *"Babylon is fallen, is fallen; and all the graven images of her gods he hath broken unto the ground"* (Isa. 21:9). Jeremiah further elaborated on the fall of Babylon in his lengthy description (110 verses in Jer. 50-51), saying, *"The word that the LORD spake against Babylon and against the land of the Chaldeans by Jeremiah the prophet"* (Jer. 50:1). Mixed in the system of Babylonianism is the ecumenical religion which has ensnared the kings of the earth with the promise of economic prosperity. Worldly politicians have used ecumenical religion for financial gain through the centuries, but when Satan will change ecumenical worship to Antichrist worship, the kings will abandon ecumenicalism and worship the Beast's commercialism, and thus proving the Lord Jesus' teaching. The Saviour said, *"No man can serve two masters: for either he will hate the one, and love the other; or else he will hold to the one, and despise the other. Ye cannot serve God and mammon"* (Mt. 6:24). Babylon is both a system and a city. As a system it is characterized as a harlot (cf. Rev. 17:5), and as a city it has its location *"in the land of Shinar"* (cf. Zech. 5:11). References to *"city"* and *"Babylon"* occur six times in the Scripture, namely, Isa. 14:4; Jer. 51:31; Rev. 14:8; 18:10 [2x]; and 18:21. Since the Scripture iterates the expression "is fallen" twice (cf. Isa. 21:9), this suggests the fall of both the system and the city. The angel revealed to John the vision of Babylon (Rev. 17:1-6) and its interpretation (Rev. 17:7-18).[20]

Transition: We've considered the Warning, now let's journey with John to the desert and see what he saw there:

II. The Woman to Be Judged (Rev. 17:3b-6)

A. Who She Drives (Rev. 17:3b)

• She Is Seen Driving the Wild-Beast (Antichrist)

1. A Beast of Blood (Scarlet)

2. A Beast of Blasphemy

3. A Beast Built for Battle

B. Her Description in Detail (Rev. 17:4-5)

---

[20] Thomas M. Strouse, *To the Seven Churches: A Commentary on the Apocalypse of Jesus Christ*, (Bible Baptist Theological Press, 2013), 679–681.

1. She Is Seen Decked Out to the Hilt (v. 4a)

Her adornment is similar to that of religious trappings of ritualistic churches today. While purple, scarlet, gold, precious stones, and pearls can all represent beauty and glory in relation to the true faith, here they reveal a false religion that prostitutes the truth.[21]

2. And Drinking of Defilement (v. 4b)

3. Her Designation Decrypted (v. 5)

Babylon was important not only politically but also religiously. Nimrod, who founded Babylon (Gen. 10:8–12), had a wife known as Semiramis who founded the secret religious rites of the Babylonian mysteries, according to accounts outside the Bible. Semiramis had a son with an alleged miraculous conception who was given the name Tammuz and in effect was a false fulfillment of the promise of the seed of the woman given to Eve (Gen. 3:15). Various religious practices were observed in connection with this false Babylonian religion, including recognition of the mother and child as God and of creating an order of virgins who became religious prostitutes. Tammuz, according to the tradition, was killed by a wild animal and then restored to life, a satanic anticipation and counterfeit of Christ's resurrection. Scripture condemns this false religion repeatedly (Jer. 7:18; 44:17–19, 25; Ezek. 8:14). The worship of Baal is related to the worship of Tammuz. After the Persians took over Babylon in 539 B.C., they discouraged the continuation of the mystery religions of Babylon. Subsequently the Babylonian cultists moved to

---

[21] John F. Walvoord, "Revelation," in *The Bible Knowledge Commentary: An Exposition of the Scriptures*, ed. J. F. Walvoord and R. B. Zuck, vol. 2 (Wheaton, IL: Victor Books, 1985), 970.

Pergamum (or Pergamos) where one of the seven churches of Asia Minor was located (cf. Rev. 2:12–17). Crowns in the shape of a fish head were worn by the chief priests of the Babylonian cult to honor the fish god. The crowns bore the words "Keeper of the Bridge," symbolic of the "bridge" between man and Satan. This handle was adopted by the Roman emperors, who used the Latin title Pontifex Maximus, which means "Major Keeper of the Bridge." And the same title was later used by the bishop of Rome. The pope today is often called the pontiff, which comes from pontifex. When the teachers of the Babylonian mystery religions later moved from Pergamum to Rome, they were influential in paganizing Christianity and were the source of many so-called religious rites which have crept into ritualistic churches. Babylon then is the symbol of apostasy and blasphemous substitution of idol-worship for the worship of God in Christ. In this passage Babylon comes to its final judgment.[22]

C. Her Drunkenness (Rev. 17:6)

- She Is Drunk on the Blood of God's True Believers

Transition: We've heard the warning; we've seen the harlot of idolatry; now consider:

III. The Wonderful Nature of this Judgment (Rev. 17:7-8)

A. John's Wonderment at the Woman Is Deterred (Rev. 17:7)

[22] John F. Walvoord, 970–971.

B. The World's Wonderment at the Wild-Beast Is Described (Rev. 17:8)

1. The Identity and Destiny of the Beast (v. 8a)

2. The Wonder of the Unbelieving Earth-Dwellers (v. 8b).

Transition: The Warning; the Woman, the Wonder of judgment; now let's put it all together by considering:

IV. The Words of Wisdom about this Judgment (Rev. 17:9-18)

A. The Wild-Beast Decrypted (World-Power) (Rev. 17:9-14)

- The Heads and Horns of the Beast Decrypted (World-powers)

B. The Waters Deciphered (World-Peoples) (Rev. 17:15)

C. The Woman Destroyed (City of Idolatry) (Rev. 17:16-18)

1. The World-Powers Destroy the Harlot (Rev. 17:16)

2. The Will and Words of God (Rev. 17:17)

3. The Woman's True Identity Exposed (Rev. 17:18)

> We believe that all the saved should live in such a manner as not to bring reproach upon their Savior and Lord. God commands His people to separate from all religious apostasy, all worldly and sinful pleasures, practices, and associations, and to refrain from all immodest and immoderate appearances...and...markings. (Rom. 12:1-2; 14:13; 2 Cor. 6:14-7:1; 2 Tim. 3:1-5; 1 John 2:15-17; 2 John 9-11; Lev. 19:28; 1 Cor. 6:19-20)
>
> ~ "Church Covenant," Broomfield Baptist Church Constitution and Bylaws

Conclusion:

Summary of Rev 17:

- 1st half of Tribulation - False religion flourishes in the false system called *"Babylon,"* possibly centered at Jerusalem, Rome, or at traditional Babylon on the Euphrates (or both); RELIGIOUS IDENTITY more important than GEOGRAPHICAL PHYSICAL LOCATION
- The system includes other "harlot" groups and exercises great political power/ clout
- In the middle of Tribulation - the Beast (antichrist) will see "her" as a challenge to his power and program
- With a league of 10 nations, Antichrist destroys the "harlot" system and sets himself up as "God" to be worshipped

Little children, keep yourselves from idols (1 Jn. 5:21)

CHAPTER TEN

Appendix F

Four Hallelujah's

Revelation 19:1-10

INTRODUCTION

"And he saith unto me, Write, Blessed are they which are called unto the marriage supper of the Lamb."

—Revelation 19:9.

I WOULD rather die to-night and be sure of sharing the bliss of the purified in you world of light than live for centuries with the wealth of this world at my feet, and miss the marriage supper of the Lamb. I have missed many appointments in my life, but by the grace of God I mean to make sure of that one. Why, the blessed privilege of sitting down at the marriage supper of the Lamb, to see the King in His beauty, to be forever with the Lord—who would miss it?[23]

~ D. L. Moody

MAIN THOUGHT:

---

[23] D. L. Moody, *The D. L. Moody Year Book: A Living Daily Message from the Words of D. L. Moody,* ed. Emma Moody Fitt (East Northfield, MA: The Bookstore, 1900), 165–166.

What assurance to know I rest in the arms of an all-powerful God. Alleluia, for the Lord God omnipotent reigns! Amen.

~ A. W. Tozer

SUB-INTRODUCTION: Connecting Context:

The Devil and his Vicious Whore and their temporal empire destroyed together are directly contrasted with Christ and His Virtuous Queen delivered the eternal Kingdom of God.

Chronologically, Chapter Nineteen follows Chapter Sixteen and the Seven Vial Judgments, although literarily it transitions appropriately from Chapter Eighteen. Chapter Nineteen revealed the saints in Heaven rejoicing, following the command to *"rejoice"* (cf. Rev. 18:20), and then revealed the Second Coming of Christ as He will conclude the Battle of Armageddon with His swift and judicious judgment on the Beast and his armies (Rev. 16:16-21). [Isaiah predicted the summary judgment on Satan, saying, *"In that day the LORD with his sore and great and strong sword shall punish leviathan the piercing serpent, even leviathan that crooked serpent; and he shall slay the dragon that is in the sea"* (Isa. 27:1).] The Second Coming of Christ is the bridge between the Tribulation (Rev. 6-19) and the Millennium (Rev. 20), as Daniel predicted (cf. Dan. 7:23-27). With Satan's kingdom destroyed, typified by the annihilation of the city Babylon, the armies of the world defeated, the Beast and the False prophet consigned to the Lake of Fire, and Satan bound for a thousand years, the Lord began to unfold the blessings that His Coming will bring, including the resurrection of the saints, the Millennial state, and the New Jerusalem in the Millennial and eternal states (see Rev. 20-22).[24]

I. FOUR ALLELUIA'S (REV. 19:1-8)

[24] Thomas M. Strouse, *To the Seven Churches: A Commentary on the Apocalypse of Jesus Christ*, (Bible Baptist Theological Press, 2013), 795.

A. First Two Alleluia's (Rev. 19:1-3):

Hallelujah! praise the Lord! praise God. Transliteration of the Heb. הלל, a piel imp. of 2-הָלַל, H2146 (hll) w. the suff. יָהּ (yh), a shortened form of Yahweh. The basic meaning of the vb. is "to be bright," and the causative meaning of the piel imp. means, lit., "make Yahweh bright," that is, "illuminate the Lord by casting a bright light on Him and His works!" "Praise Yahweh!" "Praise the Lord!" (Oda Hagemeyer, "Preiset Gott!" BibLeb 11 (1970):145–49; THAT; TDOT; DCH).[25]

1. Alleluia of Redemption (Rev. 19:1).

- An Ascription to the Lord Our God.

- Of What God Is Worthy? (cf., Ps. 104:35; 105:45; 106:1, 48; 111:1; 112:1; 113:1, 9; 116:19; 117:2; 135:1, 21; 146:1, 10; 147:1, 20; 148:1, 14; 149:1, 9; 150:1, 6; Jer. 20:13).

2. Alleluia of Retribution (Rev. 19:2-3).

- The Ascension of Eternal Incense of Justice.

John uses repetition to bring home the point: God is truly victorious and thus truly worthy of our praise! The phrase *for ever and ever* emphasizes the idea of completeness and permanence (compare Isaiah 34:10). The destruction of those who reject God's

[25] Cleon L. Rogers, Jr. & Cleon L Rogers III, *The New Linguistic and Exegetical Key to the Greek New Testament,* (Oaktree, 1998).

authority will be just that.[26]

- Why God Is Worthy? (cf., 2 Ki. 9:7; Ps. 79:10; Isa. 34:8-10; 66:22-24; Mk. 9:44, 46, 48; Ps. 58:10)

B. Final Two Hallelujah's (Rev. 19:4-8):

1. Alleluia of Reaffirmation (Rev. 19:4-5).

- The Leaders of Worship.

a. The Example of Their Worship (Rev. 19:4a; cf., Ps. 106:48).

For the last time in Revelation we meet the elders and the living creatures, the angelic worship leaders who in this context lead all of creation in celebration of God's justice (cf. 4:8–10; 5:8–14; 7:11–17; 11:16; 14:3; 19:4). We have come full circle back to Revelation 4–5 and the magnificent worship of the sovereign Lord, seated on his throne.[27]

b. The Exhortation to Praise (Rev. 19:4b-5; cf., Isa. 6:2-3; Lk. 2:13, 20; 19:37; 24:53; Acts 2:47; 3:8-9; Rom. 15:11).

2. Alleluia of the Reigning Almighty (Rev. 19:6-8).

---

[26] Jonathan Underwood and Ronald L. Nickelson, eds., *The KJV Standard Lesson Commentary, 2006–2007* (Cincinnati, OH: Standard Publishing, 2006), 307.

[27] J. Scott Duvall, *Revelation*, ed. Mark L. Strauss and John H. Walton, *Teach the Text Commentary Series* (Grand Rapids, MI: Baker Books, 2014), 247.

• The Participants In Worship.

a. The Sounds of Their Praise - Deafening (Rev. 19:6).

Thus John shows us why we can have courage to be faithful, even in the midst of great trouble: our God reigns over all and will always be able to deliver us. No wonder the praise from the multitude is thunderously loud! How can it be anything less?[28]

• **Note** - *...for the Lord God omnipotent reigneth* - Ingressive Aorist, Lit. "...has begun to rule" (cf., Zech. 14:9).

"And I heard as it were the voice of a great multitude... and as the voice of mighty thunderings, saying, Alleluia: for the Lord God omnipotent reigneth."

~ Revelation 19:6

I suppose the first thing to do would be to define omnipotence. It comes, of course, from omni, meaning "all," and potent, meaning "able to do and to have power." And so omnipotent means "able to do all and to have all power." It means having all the potency there is. Then we come to a second word, Almighty.... Now that means exactly the same thing as omnipotent.... Almighty means "having an infinite and absolute plenitude of power." When you use the words infinite and absolute you can only be talking about one person—God. There is only one infinite Being, because infinite means without limit. And it is impossible that there should be two beings in the universe without limit. So if there is only one, you are referring to God. Even philosophy and human reason, as little as I think of them, have to admit this.... God has power and whatever God has is without limit; therefore, God is omnipotent. God is absolute and whatever touches God or whatever God touches is absolute; therefore, God's power is infinite; God is Almighty. [AOGII072, 074] *What assurance to know I rest in the arms of an all-powerful God. Alleluia,*

---

[28] Underwood and Nickelson, 308.

for the Lord God omnipotent reigns! Amen.[29]

b. The Songs of Their Praise (Rev. 19:7-8).

i. Rejoicing in God (Rev. 19:7a; cf., 1 Pet. 1:3).

ii. The Reasons for Rejoicing (Rev. 19:7b-8).

a) Because the King Is Victorious (v. 7b; cf., Sol. 3:6-11).

b) Because His Queen Is Virtuous (v. 8).

> The resurrection of the saint will consummate the marriage union (cf. Phil. 3:20-21; I Cor. 15:51-52), and so all caught up to be with the Lord (cf. I Thes. 4:15-17) will constitute the Bride of Christ in the NT dispensation. Since NT saints are espoused to Christ awaiting resurrection and final consummation as Bride (cf. II Cor. 11:2), presumably so are the OT saints espoused to Christ (cf. Heb. 11:40) and awaiting their consummation at the end of the Tribulation (cf. Dan. 12:1-2). Therefore, all saints constitute the Bride and will await their respective consummation (NT saints at Rapture and OT saints at Resurrection). ...The divine Bridegroom is currently in espousal Contract with His Bride (the OT and NT saints), He will Consummate the marriage union of Himself with His Bride at the saints' respective resurrections, and Celebrate the wedding for a thousand years on earth.... The Bride's attire will be in marked contrast with the gaudy and garish garb of the Harlot, who will be dressed in purple, scarlet, and

---

[29] A. W. Tozer and Ron Eggert, *Tozer on the Almighty God: A 365-Day Devotional* (Chicago, IL: Moody Publishers, 2015).

gold (Rev. 17:4).[30]

Application:

We can trust God's promise to vindicate his people. Human Experience: When buying a home, one is usually required to offer an earnest payment, a kind of deposit indicating an honest intention to purchase. The payment signals to the seller that the buyer "means business." God has done much more than that for us in his promise to vindicate his people. After all, he demonstrated his commitment to this vindication in the blood of his own Son. More than that, he vindicated his Son, bringing him back from the grave. Surely, he is earnest. (See also Eph. 1:13–14.)[31]

Transition: We've heard the Four Hallelujah's, now let's heed:

II. A BLESSED BRIDAL INVITATION (REV. 19:9-10)

A. Beatitude of Blessing (Rev. 19:9):

1. The Bridal Invitation (v. 9a; cf., Matt. 22:1-14; Dan. 12:11-12; Lk. 14:15-16).

2. The Word's Authentication (v. 9b; cf., Rev. 22:17).

- "See Gen. 7:1, Isa. 55:1, and Mt. 11:28, for the Lord's perpetual invitation to come to Him." ~ Dr. Thomas Strouse

---

[30] Thomas Strouse, 809-810.

[31] J. Scott Duvall, 249.

B. Mistaking the Messenger (Rev. 19:10):

1. John's Mistake (v. 10a).

2. Jesus' Martyrs (v. 10b).

- Could John be longing for his martyred brother James here?

CONCLUSION

Our song will be Alleluia: for the Lord God omnipotent reigneth. What a shouting time we will have in Heaven. Folks who don't believe in shouting and praising God will have to make some adjustment when they get to glory. Dr. Harold B. Sightler said: "You know, sometimes I get rather amused at people in this life when somebody becomes excited about the Lord or somebody dares to shout the praises of the Lord. Folk will say, that is not being reverent, and I think that we need to be quiet. Let us enter into the house of God in silence, and I do not think that you ought to make much noise and commotion and become so emotional about salvation. Well, my friend, have you ever thought that when you go to heaven, **heaven is not going to be a quiet place.** The quietest world you will ever live in is this one, and when you get to heaven, you are going to hear many people saying, Hallelujah, to the top of their voices. And not only will you hear many people saying, Hallelujah, but you are going to be one of them yourself. You might have never shouted in this world. You may live a lifetime and never praise God outwardly in this world, but there is one thing for sure. *When you go to heaven and see the salvation, and the glory, and the honour, and the power of the Lord our God,* *you are going to [shout] like all the others...* " What a blessing as we read this passage and realize that those of us who are upon earth now and are redeemed through faith in the Lord Jesus Christ, whose sins are blotted out and paid for by the precious blood of Christ, will be part of that great multitude and will join in singing and worshipping God. The LORD reigneth; let the earth rejoice; let the multitude of isles be glad thereof. (Psalm 97:1)[32]

"Let every thing that hath breath praise the LORD. Praise ye the LORD." ~ Psalm 150:6

"What assurance to know I rest in the arms of an all-powerful God. Alleluia, for the Lord God omnipotent reigns! Amen."

~ A. W. Tozer

[32] Dr. Glen Jr. Spencer, *The Expository Pulpit Series: Revelation* (WORDsearch, 2013), Re 19:1–6.

www.ingramcontent.com/pod-product-compliance
Lightning Source LLC
LaVergne TN
LVHW010934110826
845149LV00013B/2602

* 9 7 9 8 9 9 2 5 4 4 0 0 8 *